LITTLE BOOK OF
BEECHING

Robin Jones

LITTLE BOOK OF
BEECHING

First published in the UK in 2013

© Demand Media Limited 2013

www.demand-media.co.uk

Printed and bound in China

ISBN 978-1-909217-59-1

Contents

Introduction

Despite the fact that Britain invented the steam railway and introduced it to the rest of the world, surprisingly few of the names associated with this globe-shaping transport technology have become commonplace household words well outside the domains of the enthusiast and historian.

RIGHT Dr Richard Beeching, British Railways chairman 1961-65

Among the elite group that have clearly managed this feat are Flying Scotsman, Stephenson's Rocket (no – despite the widespread popular misconception, George Stephenson did not invent the steam railway locomotive, that was down to Richard Trevithick), maybe Royal Scot, if only because of the marketing of the biscuit brand, perhaps Mallard, officially the world's fastest locomotive, and, dare I say it, Thomas the little blue engine. Another name that can be added to this list is that of Dr Richard Beeching.

Former British Railways chairman Dr Beeching has long been popularly portrayed as an axe-wielding ogre who closed as many railways as he could, got rid of the universally-loved steam engines and left communities all over Britain with no access to trains.

Indeed, a mistake often made in print is referring to a particular branch line as a 'Beeching closure' when he had nothing at all to do with it, the particular withdrawal of services taking place before his appointment to the British Railway Board in 1961.

Many people still hold the view that if the dreaded doctor had not descended

INTRODUCTION

RIGHT A railway official with the withdrawal of services notice at Wellingborough London Road on 29 April 1964

on the nation's railways in the sixties, many of the closed lines would still be running today. Some of the more informed among us have from the start seriously questioned the criteria used by him and those that came afterwards to justify the closure of individual routes, particularly those serving large centres of population.

Mountains of hindsight are regularly expressed with the aim of expressing the view that Beeching was wrong in this or that case, that route closures were premature, and if only the powers that be had foreseen the expansion of rural communities in commuter belt country, and the nightmarish road congestion from the 1980s onwards, in which households on even very modest incomes support two or maybe three second-hand cars, the decisions regarding the wholesale pruning of the rail network in the sixties may have been very different.

In several, though by no means all, of these 'lost line' scenarios, it is difficult not to sympathise or agree wholeheartedly, but it is so easy to pass judgement long after the event, without looking at the circumstances that prevailed at the time when many hard decisions were made.

Coming into the sector from a purely business point of view, in 1963 he produced a report, The Reshaping of British Railways, which became one of the seminal documents of British railway history.

It led to the closure of around a third of the nation's railway network, throwing tens of thousands of railwaymen on to the dole queue, disenfranchising some of the country's biggest towns from train services as well as country branches lines, in a vain bid to cut the soaring British Railways deficit in an age where passenger numbers dwindled as car ownership ran rampant. On the other hand, it also streamlined the network in a way that helped ensure its survival into the 21st century, an era in which passenger numbers are now at their highest for many decades.

So was Beeching a villain – or a hero? The story of the man who probably had the biggest impact on the nation's railways since George and Robert Stephenson invented Rocket is outlined in this special publication to mark the 50th anniversary of his controversial appointment.

Robin Jones

The road
back to roads

The essence of the postwar controversy about rail closures has its roots long before Dr Richard Beeching, and might be considered to date back to the birth of the steam locomotive itself.

Cornish mining engineer Richard Trevithick, frustrated at his home county's isolation from the canal network which provided the trade arteries of the Industrial Revolution, and indeed the poor communications between Cornwall and the rest of Britain apart from by sea, followed up earlier rudimentary experiments with horseless carriages by building his own steam locomotive – but one which would run on roads. Trevithick and engineer Andrew Vivian built a steam road carriage which, on

LEFT Richard Trevithick and engineer Andrew Vivian constructed a steam road carriage which ascended Camborne Hill in Cornwall under its own power on Christmas Eve 1801. Delighted watchers jumped aboard, making it the world's first motor car – and it emerged at least a year before the first self-propelled railway locomotive! The Trevithick Society's replica is pictured at the Railfest 200 event in 2004 at the National Railway Museum in York.

Christmas Eve 1801, climbed Camborne Hill under its own power. Onlookers jumped aboard for a ride – and so was born the world's first motor car!

The obvious advantage of road transport over rail is its great versatility. It does not rely on the provision of railway tracks and offers almost infinite personal choice and freedom for travel.

However, back in the early 19th century, the great Roman art of road-building had largely been forgotten and in those days before the invention of Tarmacadam, most of them were muddy potholed affairs which even horses and carts found uncomfortable.

In 1802, Trevithick demonstrated his pioneer London Steam Carriage in the capital, offering trips from the city centre to Paddington and back, with up to eight guests on board. It was the world's first motor bus, and the first official public run of a self-powered passenger vehicle.

However, steering was the big problem and the carriage ended up crashing into railings. The fault lay not with the vehicle, but with the poor bumpy roads.

Trevithick built a second carriage for London in 1803. Standing 13ft high, it proved too big and could not compete economically with the horse-drawn versions.

He finally overcame the problem of inadequate roads by using rails on which to run his steam locomotives. In 1802, he built a steam railway locomotive for private use at Coalbrookdale ironworks in Shropshire, and two years later gave the world's first public demonstration of one on the Penydarren Tramroad near Merthyr Tydfil.

Had the roads of the day been capable of carrying his road steam locomotives, would there have been any point in him looking at rail?

Nevertheless, the world at large was slow on the uptake of Trevithick's locomotives. The shortage of horses caused by the army needing so many for the Napoleonic Wars led to mine owners in the north of England looking for alternative traction for their private tramways in the early part of the decade that followed; but it was not until 1825 that the world's first public steam-operated railway, the Stockton & Darlington, opened, and even then locomotives were at first used for freight, with horses pulling passenger trains.

It was Rocket's triumph in the Rainhill Trials of 1829 and the Liverpool & Manchester Railway's adoption of steam locomotive traction that finally steered the railway concept on the course to transport supremacy and opened the floodgates for the years of railway mania, in which a multitude of speculative schemes sought to connect city with city, town with town, and in carving up the British mainland, created the basis of the national network for the centuries that followed.

The railways linked industrial centres to ports, facilitated the development of dormitory towns and commuter belts, took farming produce to national markets and opened up the seaside to mass tourism, among many other benefits too many to mention here. They made it easier for country folk to migrate to the expanding cities in search of a better life. In Victorian times, the railway not only reshaped society but became a backbone of it.

Expanded to its limits

By and large, the railway network had expanded to its maximum size by the dawn of the 20th century. Towards the end of Victorian times, efforts were made to connect the remaining parts of the country not deemed profitable enough to warrant attention from the major railway operators to the national network.

The Light Railways Act 1896 was a response to the economic downturn of the previous decade that had hit agri-culture and rural communities hard. It made it far easier to build a rural railway 'on the cheap' without having to apply for a costly Act of Parliament. The act limited weights to a maximum of 12 tons on each axle and line speeds to a maximum of 25mph.

Such limitations allowed the use of lightly laid track and relatively modest bridges in order to keep costs down. Also, level crossings did not have to have gates, just cattle grids.

The act led to nearly 30 local stand-ard and narrow gauge railways being built under its powers, the best-known examples perhaps being the Kent & Sussex Light Railway, which opened in 1900, the Basingstoke and Alton Light Railway of 1901, the Vale of Rheidol Railway in 1902, the Welshpool & Llanfair Light Railway in 1903 and the Leek & Manifold Valley Light Railway and the Tanat Valley Light Railway of 1904.

By contrast, in 1899, under railway magnate Edward Watkin, the Manchester, Sheffield & Lincolnshire Railway opened its 'London Extension' from Annesley, north of Nottingham, to Marylebone and changed its name to the Great Central Railway.

It was the last trunk railway to be built in Britain until the Channel Tunnel Rail Link from St Pancras International a century later; indeed, it was Watkin's intention for it to link up with a proposed Channel Tunnel, and accordingly it was built to continental loading clearances to allow potential through running of trains to and from Europe.

Also in 1899, the Great Western Railway obtained an Act of Parliament permitting construction of a double-track railway between Honeybourne and Cheltenham and doubling of the

single-track route from Stratford-upon-Avon to Honeybourne. This would link in with the North Warwickshire Line being built from Tyseley to Stratford via Bearley Juntion to provide a through route from the Midlands to the south west to compete with the Midland Railway route via the Lickey Incline.

Work began on construction of the Honeybourne-Cheltenham line in November in 1902, and it was opened throughout four years later.

In 1910, the first through trains over the route between Wolverhampton, Birmingham and the West Country and Cardiff were introduced. It may be considered as the last great cross-country route to be completed.

Railway building did not end there, but new lines that were subsequently opened were very much local affairs, such as the North Devon & Cornwall Junction Light Railway, which made use of existing mineral lines to link Halwill Junction to Torrington from 27 July 1925.

However, history recorded that, in short, virtually everywhere that was going to be connected to the rail network had been reached by Edwardian times.

LEFT The Kent & East Sussex Railway may be regarded as the epitome of the cut-price rural lines built under the 1896 Light Railways Act, with basic infrastructure and low construction costs. The Act began the last swathe of railway building before the emergence of motor transport. A special from London Victoria via the main line connection at Robertsbridge is seen arriving at Tenterden, heading by LBSCR 'Terrier' tank No 32670, with sister DS680 Waddon on the rear

The big threat emerges

The improvements in roads made in Britain following the development of the 'Macadam' type of surface pioneered by Scotsman John Loudon McAdam around 1820 led to renewed interest by inventors in looking at self-propelled forms of transport that could run over them.

The International Exposition of Electricity in Paris held in November 1881 saw French inventor Gustave Trouvé demonstrate a working three-wheeled automobile powered by electricity.

German engineer Karl Benz is generally hailed as the inventor of the modern car.

He constructed a three-wheeled carriage-like road vehicle powered by his own four-stroke cycle gasoline engine in Mannheim in 1885, and the following year his company, Benz & Cie, was granted a patent. The company began to sell automobiles off its production line in 1888, and sold around 25 of them between then and 1893, when his first four-wheeler appeared.

In 1896, Benz designed and patented the first internal-combustion flat engine, and by the end of the century, was the world's largest automobile company.

The first design for an American automobile with a gasoline internal combustion engine was produced by George Selden of New York in 1877.

In Britain, Thomas Rickett tried a production run of steam cars in 1860. Charles Santler of Malvern is regarded as having built the first petrol-powered car in the country in 1894, but it was a one-off. The first production automobiles in Britain came from the Daimler Motor Company in 1897.

Industrial-scale car production began in the USA in 1902, at the Oldsmobile plant in Lansing, Michigan. Henry

Ford's Model T came on the scene in 1908, and soon his Detroit factory was turning out cars at 15-minute intervals. Not only that, but he had also made the car affordable: by 1914, when 250,000 Model Ts had been sold, an assembly line worker could buy a Model T with four months' pay.

Ford Britain was founded in 1911 and in 1921, Citroen became the first European car manufacturer to adopt Ford's ground-breaking production line methods. By 1930, all manufacturers had followed suit, and while it was at first much regarded as a rich man's plaything, with railway travel the primary option for much of the population, car ownership was very much in the ascendancy.

Competing against itself

A railway company does not necessarily imply that it exists to promote the railway concept; the key word is 'company', a body that is created to generate profits by the best means possible.

When the dawn of the 20th century saw that motor road vehicles would shape the future of transport later if not sooner, the Great Western Railway

looked at providing bus services not only as a feeder to its train services, but also as a cheaper alternative to building new branch lines in sparsely populated rural areas which would never pay. The GWR baulked at the idea of spending £85,000 on extending the Helston branch with a light railway to Britain's southernmost village, Lizard Town, and decided to try motor buses instead.

Two vehicles that had been used temporarily by the Lynton & Barnstaple Railway were acquired, the service was launched 17 August 1903, the summer before City class 4-4-0 No 3440 City of Truro unofficially became the first steam locomotive in the world to break the 100mph barrier, with a speed of 102.3mph recorded hauling the 'Ocean Mails Special' from Plymouth to Paddington on 9 May 1904.

The idea of a railway company running a motor bus dated back to 1890, when the Belfast & Northern Counties Railway fitted seats to a petrol-engined parcels delivery van and took fares for rides in it.

The Lizard buses proved so popular and profitable that other routes were soon established, first locally to Mullion, Ruan Minor and Porthleven, and then further afield at Penzance.

A bus route from Slough station to Beaconsfield was launched on 1 March 1904, followed by routes to Windsor on 18 July that year. Indeed, the first GWR double deckers appeared on the Slough-Windsor service in 1904 onwards.

A route from Wolverhampton to Bridgnorth was briefly operated from 7 November 1904 using steam buses, motor buses replacing them the following year.

By the end of 1904, 36 buses were in GWR operation, and the Great Western Railway (Road Transport) Act was passed in 1928; the GWR boasted the biggest railway bus fleet. This act paved the way for the services to be trans-

LEFT Great Western Railway motor bus No 1278

FAR LEFT Poster advertising the start of GWR bus services from Helston to Lizard Town on 17 August 1903, an experiment which began as an alternative to building a railway line and rapidly evolved into a competitor to rail services

ferred to bus companies, although the railway was to be a shareholder in these operations. On 1 January 1929, the GWR routes in Devon and Cornwall went over to the new Western National Omnibus Company, 50 per cent owned by the railway and the other half by the National Omnibus and Transport Company. That year the GWR acquired 30 per cent of the shares in the Devon General Omnibus and Touring Company.

The final bus services operated by the GWR began in the Weymouth area in 1935, jointly run with the London & South Western Railway, and were transferred to Southern National on 1 January 1934.

Never afraid to compete with the railway concept, on 11 April 1933, the GWR launched its first air service, flying from Cardiff to Exeter and Plymouth.

The GWR and the other major railway operators built up extensive fleets of lorries and vans to supplement rail freight services. Yet what would happen when the day came that road vehicles would no longer supplement goods trains, but carry freight from start to finish in their own right?

Road freight on the rise

Britain would never be the same after World War One. One of the marked changes was the blurring of the distinction between social classes: public schoolboys and labourers alike had experienced the horrors of the Western Front together, and never again would it be a case of one doffing their cap to the other. Similarly, churchgoing rapidly declined after 1918, with religion becoming less relevant to a population bemused at why it had not been able to prevent the carnage of the trenches.

There was a fresh spirit of entrepreneurship among the soldiers returning from the front. Large quantities of road vehicles became sold off as military surplus, and many were eagerly bought up by those wishing to launch their own haulage businesses. In doing so, freight was switched slowly but surely from rail to the cheaper and more versatile road alternative.

In turn, local authorities began to build more roads to cater for the increase in traffic.

Because of the growth of road haulage, the railways' profit margins began to suffer. The road hauliers could offer significantly lower prices than the railways, while offering the benefits of door-to-door delivery, while the railways were hampered by their original charters of the 1840s and 50s to act as common carriers, and legally were unable to refuse unprofitable cargoes and lower their transportation costs accordingly.

A series of Royal Commissions into the problem was held in the 30s, but failed to find a solution. Chancellor of the Exchequer Neville Chamberlain, who as Prime Minister is best known for his 'peace in our time' appeasement of Hitler, increased vehicle excise duty, leaving the hauliers paying all of the Annual Road Fund. This was a big boost to the railways, who were now theoretically back in the driving seat, but before they could reap big dividends from it, World War Two broke out. Furthermore, the railways were not released from their historic

common carrier obligations until 1957.

Dr Beeching did not invent main line railway closures: that was a process that may be deemed to have begun more than a century before he came on the transport scene. In 1851, the Newmarket & Chesterford Railway closed its Great Chesterford to Six Mile Bottom section after opening a more viable length linking Six Mile Bottom straight to Cambridge.

World War One saw a comparatively small number of rural railways closed, with their tracks lifted for use on the Western Front military lines, never to reopen again. These included the Bideford, Westward Ho! & Appledore

LEFT The surviving buildings of Whitwick station on the Charnwood Forest Railway, and early standard gauge closure

FAR LEFT While rail technology had reached the point where steam locomotives broke the 100mph barrier, as was said to have happened with GWR 4-4-0 No 3440 City of Truro in 1904, buses were already emerging as a potential competitior. City of Truro, now owned by the National Railway Museum and restored in time for the centenary of the unofficial record-breaking run, is seen at Horse Cove between Dawlish and Teignmouth with Pathfinder Tours' 'Ocean Mail 100' tour from Kingswear to Bristol on 10 May 2004

THE CORONATION SCOT
ASCENDING SHAP FELL
by Norman Wilkinson, P.R.I.

LMS

The Coronation Scot, blue and silver express of the L M S Railway, runs each weekday (except Saturdays) between London and Glasgow in 6½ hours, leaving Euston Station and Central Station at 1·30 p.m. The trains consist of nine air-conditioned coaches, internally panelled in decorative woods. The locomotive Coronation Scot (No. 6220) is one of five high-speed streamlined engines designed to maintain high average speeds in all weathers over the famous West Coast Route to Scotland, which includes such difficult ascents as Shap Fell (915 ft.), and Beattock Summit (1,014 ft.). Coronation Scot attained on a test run with the train in 1937 a maximum speed of 114 miles an hour, creating a British railway record.

ABOVE Many view the 30s as the zenith of Britain's railway network. This poster advertises the classic 'Coronation Scot', a named luxury streamlined express passenger train of the London, Midland & Scottish Railway

Railway, and the GWR line from Rowington to Henley-in-Arden, which had been superseded by the North Warwickshire Line, but were still very much small beer in the overall scheme of railways.

The 1930s, however, saw a swathe of closures of many 'rural fringe' lines, the like of which had been empowered by the 1896 Light Railways Act. Some, like the GWR-run Welshpool & Llanfair and Corris railways, lost their passenger services but remained open for freight, while others, like the Lynton & Barnstaple, by then part of the Southern Railway, the Welsh Highland Railway and the Leek & Manifold Valley Railways, closed outright.

The standard gauge Charnwood Forest Railway in Leicestershire ceased running passenger trains in 1931, and Birmingham's Harborne branch closed to passengers in 1934 in the face of direct competition from trams and motor buses.

The Weston, Clevedon & Portishead Railway, the only direct route of any description between those three towns, ran its last public train in 1940.

Few of these can be regarded as mainstays of the railway network; indeed, regardless of their historical or romantic appeal, it is debatable whether some of them should have been built at all, and once the motor road vehicle provided a creditable alternative, it is all but certain that they would not have been. In any event, so many of the 1896 Act railways had a lifespan of only around three decades, and their demise gave a strong pointer to the future of rural lines.

The 'Big Four' become one

The big watershed in the history of Britain's railways in 1948 came when the national network was taken into permanent public ownership for the first time.

The nation's railways had been placed under state control during World War One, and it was clear that the network could be run more efficiently with fewer operators. Afterwards there were calls for complete nationalisation – a move first mooted in 1850. However, the Railways Act 1921 provided a compromise with the grouping of most of the country's 120 railway companies into four main ones. These were the 'Big Four' comprising the Great Western Railway, the London, Midland & Scottish Railway, the London & North Eastern Railway and the Southern Railway.

World War Two again saw the nation's railways acting as one company, a time when network saw more use than at any other point in its history.

Luftwaffe air raids inflicted heavy damage, particularly around London and Coventry, while the diversion of resources from maintenance led to the network falling into disrepair. After the war, it was soon realised that the private sector could not afford to put right the damage and decay, and so Clement Attlee's Labour government decided to nationalise the railways under the Transport Act 1947. British Railways came into existence

ABOVE A poster being
displayed in 1947
informing the public
that the country's
railways were to be
nationalised. This
is part of a display
in the Great Hall of
the National Railway
Museum

as the business name of the Railway Executive of the British Transport Commission.

It was clear from the start that there would be closures. The Railway Executive was fully aware that some lines on the very dense network were unprofitable and also difficult to justify on social grounds. Going back to the Victorian era of Railway Mania, it is easy to argue to that many lines, particularly local branches, were built that history was to show could never really be justified. In terms of long-distance travel, there soon arose competition between different companies for the

LITTLE BOOK OF **BEECHING**

same passengers. One famous example was the 'Races to the North' whereby rivals competed to see who could take passengers from London to Scotland fastest, while the GWR and London & South Western Railway, later Southern Railway, competed strongly for the London-Exeter-Plymouth markets, as did the GWR and LMS for London-Birmingham, to quote another of many examples. While such rival routes served different communities along the way, if inter-city travel was considered of paramount important, then a logical step forward would be to pick the best route and divert all the resources to that, and maybe considering the other for closure.

The first official closure under British Railways was the goods-only line from Mantle Lane East to the foot of Swannington Incline in Leicestershire, by the new London Midland Region, in February 1948. The first passenger services to be withdrawn were those from Woodford & Hinton station on the Great Central route, to Byfield on the Stratford & Midland Juntion Railway, on 31 May 1948, also by the LMR.

Another of the very early closures was that of the 2ft 3in gauge Corris Railway,

inherited from the GWR, which was axed following flood damage of 21 August 1948.

The following year, the British Transport Commission set up the Branch Lines Committee, with a remit to close the least-used branch lines.

The modest programme of closures continued in 1949 with passenger services withdrawn from Liverpool Lime Street to Alexandra Dock, Stratford-upon-Avon to Broom, and Fenchurch Street to Stratford (Bow Juntion).

In 1950, a total of 150 route miles were closed, rising to 275 in 1951 and 300 in 1952.

BELOW The Northern Eastern railway branch line north of Tow Law to Blackhill in County Durham lost its passenger service as early as May 1939. The line south from Tow Law to Crook closed on 11 June 1956. LNER A5 4-6-2T No 69836 is seen with a passenger train at Tow Law in the early fifties

The Marples master plan

RIGHT Harold 'Supermac' Macmillan opened Britain's first motorway, the Preston bypass later part of the M6

FAR RIGHT Minister of Transport Ernest Marples discusses the M1, Britain's first motorway (M1) with Sir Owen Williams, when opening the 72-mile road

The October 1959 General Election saw the appointment of Ernest Marples as Minister of Transport. Marples joined the Government in 1957 as Postmaster General, and introduced the subscriber trunk dialling telephone system which made redundant the use of operators on national telephone calls. He also introduced postcodes to the UK. On 2 June 1957, he started the first draw for the then-new Premium Bonds savings scheme.

He served as Transport Minister until 16 October 1964, during which time he introduced brought in parking meters, yellow lines and seat belts.

Marples, a qualified accountant, was undeniably a roads man: indeed, he had founded Marples-Ridgway, a construction firm that built many roads, and was to quickly demonstrate that preferred expenditure on motorways to investment in railways. For in 1959, he gave the green light for the first inter-city British motorway, the M1. Britain's first section of motorway, the eight-mile Preston bypass, the first part of the M6 to be completed, was opened on 5 December 1958. It was built after two years of work, without modern hydraulic machinery, and was officially opened by Prime Minister Harold Macmillan, whose car led a convoy along it.

Former bridge engineer Harry Yeadon, 86, later recalled: "People recognised the significance. It was a guinea pig for all the future motorways and a lot of innovation went into its design and construction."

Indeed, it was a massive pointer if there was one, to future national transport trends and policies. Motorways had first been introduced in Italy by Benito Mussolini in the 1920s and then in Germany in 1931, Hitler subsequently speeding up the development programme. In Britain, Lord Montagu had formed a company to build a 'motorway like road' from London to Birmingham in 1923, but it was not

M1

until the Special Roads Act 1949 that the construction of roads limited to a limited vehicle classifications was allowed, and the 1950s when the country's first motorways were given the Government go-ahead.

When the Preston bypass was opened, it had solid shale either side instead of hard shoulders, and if you broke down and tried to change a wheel, the jack sunk into the ground. But it would not remain that way for long.

The first section of the M1, between Junction 5 (Watford) and Junction 18 (Crick/Rugby) was opened by Marples on 2 November 1959 in a short cer-emony that took place near Slip End, at Junction 10 south of Luton. It has been said that when cars waiting at the Junction to be among the first to travel on the new road poured down the slip road, the recently-appointed Transport Minister said: "My God, what have I started!"

He expressed concern about cars not been driven in a safe manner, but it was not until 1965 that the 70mph speed limit on motorways was introduced.

To avoid a conflict of interest, Marples undertook to sell his control-ling shareholder interest in his road construction company as soon as he

became Transport Minister, although there was a purchaser's requirement that he buy back the shares after he ceased to hold office, at the original price, should the purchaser so require. It was later revealed that he had sold his shares to his wife.

It was therefore ironic that the man who held the future of the railways in his hands should be so closely connected with a major financial interest in road building.

As Transport Minister, his first move was to impose tighter control over the British Transport Commission and call a halt to the excesses of the modernisation programme.

Early in 1960, the BTC was told that any investment project that involved spending more than £250,000 would have to be cleared with the Ministry, the ultimate decision resting with Marples.

By then, there was a widespread feeling at Whitehall that railways were an expensive and increasingly outmoded legacy from Victorian times, and why should the national network be propped up with large amounts of taxpayer's money when roads were being built to do the same job and more effectively?

The slow pruning of the most unprofitable fringes of the railway network had steadily continued throughout the fifties. In 1953, 275 miles were axed, followed by around 500 miles between 1954-57, and just 150 miles in 1958.

The shock to a system

The biggest shock in transport circles came that year, when the closure of a complete system was recommended by a British Railways committee.

On 28 February 1959, the Midland & Great Northern Joint Railway lines closed, apart from a few piecemeal sections like Cromer to Melton Constable. At the Grouping of 1923, the M&GN had been Britain's largest joint railway with 186 route miles, penetrating from the Midlands a junction with the Midland Railway at Saxby into East Anglia where the Great Eastern Railway had otherwise enjoyed a monopoly. It served Great Yarmouth, Norwich and King's Lynn.

The M&GN system was formally operationally incorporated into the LNER in 1936, although it relied heavily dependent on the LMS to provide the bulk of its longer-distance traffic including many holiday excursion trains from the Midlands and the north.

Largely single track, in the years following nationalisation it had appeared increasingly vulnerable: a harbinger of doom was the withdrawal of all night goods trains after February 1953.

BATTLE OF THE ROADS

The brutal, stark story

Published by the Daily Mirror   One shilling and sixpence

GREAT LITTLE CARS

MORRIS MINI-MINORS

Early in 1958 there were rumours that closures were on their way, but many were left breathless when the full scale of them became apparent. The whole system was listed among the 350 route miles nationwide to be closed in 1959, the only sections to be left open for passenger traffic were Sheringham to Melton Constable and North Walsham to Mundesley. For the time being, goods trains only were allowed to continue to Rudham from King's Lynn, between Spalding and Bourne, and Spalding and Sutton Bridge.

One reason given was that West Lynn Bridge over the River Great Ouse needed major repairs to its structure, but many saw at the time and still believe today that this was more of an excuse than a reason.

At midnight on 28 February 1959, most of the M&GN system closed. At 8am the following Monday, rail connections at Sutton Bridge were severed and lifting of the track to South Lynn begun in earnest, followed by the demolition of West Lynn Bridge which meant that there could be no going back. The Yarmouth Beach station building was ripped apart, the site becoming a coach station, and by January 1960

Last summer: Midland 3F 0-6-0 No 44231 passes the Midland & Great Northern signal bracket as it crosses the River Great Ouse at South Lynn with the 8am Chesterfield to Yarmouth Beach train on 30 August 1958

ABOVE September 1960 sees an AA motorway patrol in full wet weather gear load a broken down car on the hard shoulder of the M1 onto the AA's new 'retriever unit' for recovery on the back of his Land Rover

the track had been lifted as far as Potter Heigham.

Much of the M&GN rail traffic transferred to former GER lines.

The message to railwaymen was short, sharp and simple: if a complete system could be eradicated overnight, where would the powers that be stop in their drive to stem the losses at all costs?

It was not only on British Railways where steel wheels had been replaced by rubber tyres. In Britain's cities, the street trams which had brought cheap fast transport in the early 20th century had by then all but been phased out,

along with the slightly more versatile trolleybuses that had superseded them in many places.

London's trams ceased operation after 5 July 1952, with Birmingham closing its tramways the following year. The last closure was that of the Glasgow routes on 2 September 1962, leaving only Blackpool with trams. If they could be replaced by buses, why could they not do the job of the railways for people who could not afford a car?

In 1960, one in nine families was said to own a car: that figure seems laughable by today's standards, but, coming three years after Prime Minister Harold Macmillan told Conservative party supporters in Bedford: "Most of our people have never had it so good", it indicated the results of the 1950s wave of prosperity. There were also around 1.9-million motorbikes at the time, again highlighting the prevalence of private transport as an alternative to the railways.

On 10 March 1960, at the start of the parliamentary debate on the above-mentioned Guillebaud Report on rail-waymen's wages, Macmillan said: "The carriage of minerals, including coal, an important traffic for the railways, has gone down. At the same time, there has been an increasing use of road transport in all its forms.

"The industry must be of a size and pattern suited to modern conditions and prospects. In particular, the railway system must be remodelled to meet current needs, and the modernisation plan must be adapted to this new shape.

"Secondly, the public must accept the need for changes in the size and pattern of the industry. This will involve certain sacrifices of convenience, for example, in the reduction of uneconomic ser-vices."

His words were music indeed to the ears of the Road Haulage Association, but struck a note that would reverberate throughout the railway industry in the years to come, to the anger of users and staff across the nation.

Yes, cutbacks are needed, but what about subsidies?

Around this time, a report compiled by the Parliamentary Select Committee stated that "there is no doubt that a large-scale British railway system can be profitable."

It emphasised that the size and shape of the system must depend primar-ily on financial considerations, but Government subsidies for essential but unprofitable services were recom-mended.

The committee added that direct prof-itability was not the only consideration. Because of the cost of road building and congestion on them, the national inter-est may require railway services which do not directly pay for themselves, but which may cost the country less than the alternatives. There are several routes, like the Midland & Great Northern, for which the future may appear to be

LEFT Pointing the way to the future: at Broughton flyover on the M1, near Newport Pagnell (now junction 14), a senior AA manager appears to be inspecting the new motorway patrol force, outside the organisation's new mobile motorway control centre

ABOVE The last London tram arrives at New Cross depot on 5 July 1952 packed with passengers

uncertain, but which might be removed from the "closure list" if such recommendations were adopted.

It was clear, however, that if subsidies are to be paid, the case for their retention must be fully proven, the report said.

Meanwhile, an independent advisory panel chaired by industrialist Sir Ivan Stedeford had been appointed to examine the structure and finances of the British Transport Commission.

Among its members was a Dr Richard Beeching, a physicist and engineer at Imperial Chemical Industries who had been recommended by Sir Frank Smith, ICI's former Chief Engineer.

Following the panel's recommendations, Marples presented a White Paper to Parliament in December 1960, calling for the splitting of the British Transport Commission into a number of bodies, with the railways being run by the new British Railways Board. It also set financial targets for the railways, which would lead to cuts.

The paper read: "Sweeping changes will be needed. Effort and sacrifices will be required from all. The public will have to be prepared to face changes in the extent and nature of the services, provided and, when necessary, in the prices charged for them. The taxpayer will have to face a major capital reorganisation as well as continue to carry a large part of the burden until the railways are paying their way again. Those working in these undertakings, if their livelihood is to be assured, will have to play their part in increasing productivity and enabling the labour force to be deployed so as to secure maximum efficiency in operation.

"The heart of the problem is in the railways. They are a great national enterprise and a vital basic industry. They employ half a million people and represent an investment of nearly £1600-million, which is growing by more than £100-million each year. A railway system of the right size is an essential element in our transport network and will remain so for as long as can be foreseen. The development of other forms of transport and new

techniques now faced British Railways, like the railways in other countries, with problems of competition and adaptation to modern circumstances and public demand.

"The railways are now in a grave financial plight. They are a long way short (by about £60-million a year) of covering even their running costs. This is quite apart from the problem of meeting their interest charges, whether upon the price paid for the undertakings or upon the money since borrowed for modernisation and other purposes. These interest charges now total some £75-million a year.

"The practical test for the railways, as for other transport, is how far the users are prepared to pay economic prices for the services provided. Broadly, this will in the end settle the size and pattern of the railway system. It is already clear that the system must be made more compact. There must also be modernisation, not only of lay-out, equipment and operating methods, but of organisation and management structure."

The break-up of the BTC was facilitated by the Transport Act 1962. Despite brief encouraging figures around the turn of the decade, in 1961 the railways' annual loss on operating account reached nearly £87-million.

On 15 March 1961, Marples told the House of Commons that Dr Richard Beeching would become the first chairman of the new British Railways Board, from 1 June that year.

Chapter 3

Cometh the hour, cometh the axeman

Few members of the general public had cause to know the name of Richard Beeching until that time. Beeching was born in Sheerness on the Isle of Sheppey, the second of four brothers. His father was a reporter with the Kent Messenger, his mother a schoolteacher and his grandfather on his mother's side a dockyard worker.

Soon after he was born, the Beeching family moved to Maidstone. All four boys attended the local Church of England primary school, Maidstone All Saints, and won scholarships to Maidstone Grammar School. Richard was appointed as a prefect there, although while his three brothers loved cricket, he preferred to go for walks in the countryside.

Richard and Geoffrey Beeching both read physics at London's Imperial College of Science & Technology in London and graduated with first class honours degrees. There, Richard completed a research doctorate under the supervision of Sir George Thomson, the Nobel laureate in physics who achieved fame through his joint discovery of the wave properties of the electron by electron diffraction, and who was knighted in 1943.

Richard Beeching remained in research, taking up a post at London's Fuel Research Station in Greenwich in 1936 and then, the following year, moving to the Mond Nickel Laboratories. There, he became chief physicist, carrying out research in the fields of physics, metallurgy and mechanical engineering.

ABOVE Dr Beeching on the footplate of GNR 0-6-0 saddle tank No 1247 his visit to the Bluebell Railway where he opened a station rather than closed one

He married Ella Margaret Tiley in 1938, and the pair set up home in Solihull. The pair had known each other since schooldays.

When he was 29, during World War Two, Beeching was loaned by Mond Nickel to the Ministry of Supply and worked in the armament design and research departments at Fort Halstead. There, he had a rank equivalent to that of army captain.

He worked under the department's superintendent and chief engineer Sir Frank Smith, the former chief engineer with ICI.

Richard's brother Kenneth was killed in the war.

When Smith returned to ICI after the war, his successor promoted Beeching, now 33, to deputy chief engineer with a rank equivalent to that of brigadier.

Beeching continued his work with armaments, concentrating on anti-aircraft weaponry and small arms, but in 1948 he rejoined his former boss Sir Frank Smith, as his personal technical assistant at ICI.

Zip fasteners not bombs and bullets were now the focus of Beeching's attention. He also worked paints and leather cloth, with a remit to boost efficiency and cut production costs.

During his time at ICI, he was appointed to the Terylene Council, the forerunner of the company's fibres division, the board of which he later joined.

In 1953 he accepted a posting to Canada as vice-president of ICI (Canada) Ltd and was placed in charge of a terylene plant in Ontario.

Two years later, he came back to Britain as chairman of the ICI Metals Division on Smith's recommendation.

He was appointed to the ICI board in 1957, serving as technical director, and for a brief period as development director.

It was yet another recommendation by Smith, who had by then retired, that saw Marples appoint Beeching to the previously-mentioned advisory group.

When he was given the job of chairman of British Railways, succeeding Sir

Brian Robertson, Beeching was paid an equivalent salary to that which he received at ICI, £24,000 a year, said to be around £370,000 by today's standards. That was £14,000 more than the Prime Minister was paid, and 250 per cent more than the head of any other nationalised industry received at the time. ICI gave Beeching leave of absence for five years by ICI to do the job.

Beeching's brief was simple: return the railways to profitability without delay.

In doing so, he would change the transport map of Britain forever, and for good or bad, create a new streamlined railway system out of the steam era network.

In May 1961, The Railway Magazine wrote in its leader column: "The appointment of Dr Beeching has aroused mixed feelings both inside and outside the railway service. Surprise and concern have been expressed because the choice did not fall on a senior rail-

way officer who could have brought to the new board many years of specialised experience of the intricacies of railway administration.

Dr Beeching lacks this qualification, but, as a member of the Stedeford Committee, he must be fully aware of the magnitude of his task. It may be that a man who has attained a high position in the scientific industrial world at a comparatively early age will prove equally successful in the railway sphere, and it would be unfair to prejudge the appointment."

With remarkable clarity of vision, the writer continued: "A noteworthy feature is that Dr Beeching's present intention to return to ICI after five years probably will cause him to be regarded in circles as a surgeon rather than a railwayman."

Ironically, on the same page, it was noted that the first section of the British Transport Commission's museum at Triangle Place, Clapham, London, was opened to the public on Wednesday 29 March. Apart from the then much-smaller York Railway Museum at York, it was the first permanent exhibition in Great Britain entirely devoted to history of transport by rail, road and water. Soon, much much more would be consigned to railway network, not least of all a third of the network.

In his first year in office, while drawing up the legendary blueprint which would bring him overnight fame or notoriety, depending on your perspective, Dr Beeching gained a then-unique insight into at least one controversial railway closure – by helping to reopen it!

On 1 April 1962, he travelled on a railtour from London Bridge via Haywards Heath and Ardingly to Horsted Keynes, where the network still connected with the newly-opened Bluebell Railway, behind Great Northern Railway J52 0-6-0ST No 1247, the first ex-main line steam engine to be preserved by a private individual. There, he officially opened a new halt built by the Bluebell revivalists in the form of Holywell Halt.

The British Transport Commission had intended to close the loss-making Lewes-East Grinstead line from 28 May 1955. The cross-country route engineered by the London, Brighton & South Coast Railway served mainly rural areas and was largely devoid of passengers, but that did not stop local spinster and battleaxe Madge Bessemer – who normally travelled by private car, launching a campaign to keep it open.

At first she asked for help from the Society for the Reinvigoration of Unremunerative Branch Lines in the United Kingdom, but found the nostalgia-minded organisation to be of less than no practical help.

She then studied key documents from the line's history, and reread the small print in the Act of Parliament which had empowered its building. It required the owners to run four trains each day. Missed by the BTC, she had discovered a loophole.

Helped by local MP Tufton Beamish, she forced the BTC to reinstate the service – very begrudgingly happened in August the following year. Madge, grand-daughter of Henry Bessemer, who invented the process for converting pig iron into steel with his Bessemer Converter, said: "They have got to keep the law just like everyone else!"

However, British Railways complied with the letter of the law, but not so much with the spirit of it. While four trains a day were indeed reinstated, they were mostly restricted to just a single coach, and they did not stop at Barcombe or Kingscote, because those two stations did not appear in the original Act of Parliament. Also, the ser-

LEFT Doomed before the Beeching era: Melton Mowbray North station lay on the Great Northern Railway & London & North Western Railway joint route from Nottingham (London Road) to Market Harborough, over which regular passenger services ceased on 7 December 1953. However, the lucrative summer specials, mainly from Leicester to Skegness or Mablethorpe, survived until 1962, and through goods traffic lasted until 1964. Ivatt mogul No 43066 carries a wreath of its tender on the line's last day, 5 July 1964

ABOVE A British Railways delivery truck in London in 1962. One of Beeching's biggest tasks was to make rail freight pay

vices appeared to be deliberately timed so that they would be of little use – arriving at East Grinstead after the start of normal working hours and leaving before knocking-off time.

The 'Sulky Service,' as it came to be nicknamed, kept the line alive while British Railways went to the time and trouble to obtain the necessary statutory powers for revoking the terms of the original Act.

Services were again withdrawn between Lewes and East Grinstead on 16 March 1958, but Madge Bessemer had by then attracted the ears of the national press, radio and TV to her cause. When the final train ran, the unduly large numbers of passengers and sightseers proved that the public at large really did care about rail closures.

On that last day, Madge met Chris Campbell, a part-time student at Carshalton Technical College who had many recollections of travelling on the line while spending school holidays with

relatives. Inspired by her efforts to save the line, Chris, 18, wondered if there was anything that could still be done. Elsewhere, Martin Eastland, 19, a telecommunications engineering student of Haywards Heath, David Dallimore, a student at the London School of Economics, from Woodingdean, and Brighton-based Alan Sturt, 19, who was studying at the Regent Street Polytechnic, had kicked around the idea of setting up a Lewes and East Grinstead Railway Preservation Society.

The publicity machine was sparked off again in December 1958 by a chance remark made by Chris to a reporter on the East Grinstead Observer about the formation of the preservation society, leading to the headline: "Bluebell Line Sensation – May Be Run Privately".

Chris travelled on a Rambler's Excursion from London Victoria to Horsted Keynes on 7 December, two days after the report appeared. At Horsted Keynes, his party of 15 walked south along the disused trackbed to Newick & Chailey station where they had lunch in view of Madge who was picking flowers on the lineside opposite. It was then that Chris met Martin for the first time and decided to call a public meeting

to officially launch the society.

The landmark founders' meeting was held on 15 March 1959, at the Church Lads Brigade Hall in Haywards Heath. It was chaired by one Bernard Holden because the students, all under 21, were minors in the eyes of the then law and legally barred from holding positions. Bernard, 51, a signalling assistant in the general manager's office at Liverpool Street, had been born in Barcombe station house where his father Charles was stationmaster.

The rest is history. Part of the line, between Sheffield Park and a point south of Horsted Keynes, reopened on

7 August 1960. The revivalists did not succeed in their original ambition to save the entire Lewes-East Grinstead route, but their Bluebell Railway slowly but surely grew to become a market leader in preserved steam railways.

There would be many more would-be Madge Bessemers in the decade that followed, but few would meet with even a hint of her albeit temporary success in the face of an unprecedented tidal wave of Whitehall negativity against rural railways.

As for Dr Beeching, he and his wife moved to nearby East Grinstead in the sixties and he spent the rest of his life there.

Ironically, Holywell Halt subsequently closed while the Bluebell Railway thrives!

ABOVE Not exactly the Beeching Axe of legend: Dr Beeching never had a physical axe as such but he did start off with a pair of scissors, preserved in the National Railway Museum at York. These scissors were made to mark the opening of the rebuilt Plymouth station opened by him on 26 March 1962. They were made by T Hardy & Sons that same year and were donated to the NRM by Beeching's daughter Ann Bailey

Chapter 4

The Reshaping of British Railways

The Transport Act 1962, which broke up the British Transport Commission and created the British Railways Board, set the scene for what was to quickly follow. The new board was directed under Section 22 of the Act to run the railways so that its operating profits were "not less than sufficient" for meeting the running costs.

This clause marked a major first for British railway legislation and was a turning point for the system, for from then onwards, each railway service should pay for itself or at least show that it had the possibility of doing so. The days of mass subsidy, with profitable services supporting the unprofitable ones, and the taxpayer footing the bill if the overall figures did not tally in the

LEFT The Cambrian Railways' Mid-Wales line linked Newtown, Llanidloes, Rhayader, Builth Wells and Brecon and had more than 20 intermediate stations serving sparse local populations. It closed on 31 December 1962. Ivatt 2-6-0 No 46523 is seen arriving at Llanidloes with the 5.40pm Moat Lane Junction to Builth Wells on 7 June 1960. Cars won the day here: the site is now occupied by the town's bypass

FAR LEFT Dr Richard Beeching holds up a copy of his 1963 report, The Reshaping of British Railways

right way, would soon be over, or so it was intended.

It was the Select Committee of the House of Commons on Nationalised Industries which had decided that the British Transport Commission should make its decisions exclusively on considerations of "direct profitability". Where decisions not based on self-sufficiency but "on grounds of the national economy or of social needs" had to be taken, the Minister of Transport would shoulder the responsibility.

No longer would there be a special case for the railways: they would have to compete in a free market in the same way as any other business. Section 3(1) of the Act stated that it was the duty of the British Railways Board to provide railway services with regard to "efficiency, economy and safety of operation".

The 1962 Act also introduced new legislation for the closure of railway lines. Section 56(7) demanded that British Railways gave at least six weeks notice of its intention to close a line and to publish the proposal in two local

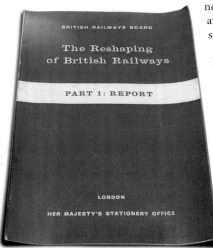

newspapers in the area affected in two successive weeks.

Each notice would have to provide the proposed closure dates, details of alternative public transport, including services which British Railways was to lay on as a result of closure and inviting objections within the six week period to a specified address.

A copy of the notice was also to be sent to the relevant Area Transport Users Consultative Committee, which would receive objections from affected rail users, and submit a report to the Minister of Transport.

The Central Transport Consultative Committee was a new body that replaced a similar one established under the Transport Act 1947 which nationalised the railways, and was intended to represent the railways' consumers.

The Area Transport Users Consultative Committees were additional bodies set up to cover local areas.

It would be the job of the Area Committees to look at the hardship which it considered would be caused as a result of the closure, and recommend measures to ease that hardship.

The line closure would not go ahead until the Area Committee had reported to the Transport Minister and he had given his consent to it. Based on the Area Committee's report, the Minister could subject his consent to closure to certain conditions, such as the provision of alternative transport services. However, the Minister was not bound to follow any of the Area Committee's recommendations, and therefore there was no safeguard by which public feeling would take priority over policy.

In December 1962, The Railway Magazine reported: "The name of Dr Beeching is likely to live on in the Leicestershire village of Countesthorpe long after the current railway troubles are forgotten. It is reported that the parish council there has agreed to name a new thoroughfare off Station Road 'Beeching Close' because residents associate him with the closure of their railway station.

Countesthorpe station, just south of Leicester on the Midland line to Rugby, had closed in February 1962. While villagers there might have been irate, they would soon have likeminded bedfellows – to the tune of many millions. The nation had not seen anything yet.

The doctor prescribes the medicine

The biggest shock to the railway system was delivered on 27 March 1963, when Dr Beeching's report, The Reshaping of British Railways, was published. Seasoned railwaymen had seen traffic dwindle to a trickle or nothing on many lines and knew that closures were inevitable; however, the publication of a report detailing sweeping changes of the extent proposed was still received by many with horror.

To members of the ordinary public, who had no grasp of railway finances, and had always accepted that the railways 'would always be there', Beeching would be immortalised as the man who took 'their' line away.

Dubbed the 'Beeching Bombshell' or the 'Beeching Axe' by the press, the 148-page report called for a third of the rail network to be closed and ripped up.

Out of around 18,000 route miles, 5000, mainly comprising cross-country routes and rural branches, should close completely, it recommended.

Not only were branches to rural backwaters listed for closure: this time, trunk routes were listed – the Somerset & Dorset Joint Railway system, the Waverley Route from Carlisle to Edinburgh, the Great Central Railway from Nottingham to Marylebone, along with passenger services on the Settle and Carlisle route.

ABOVE In a scene typical of Beeching closures and final trains, hordes of lineside photographers scramble to take a picture of Ivatt 2-6-2T No 41222 leaving Wolverton on 5 September 1964, the last day of service on the Newport Pagnell branch

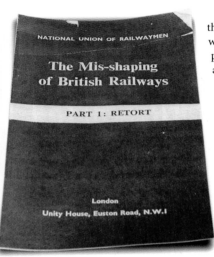

ABOVE The National Union of Railwaymen's response to Beeching's report. It was titled The Mis-Shaping of Britain's Railways

Over and above all this, many other lines were to lose their passenger services and remain open for freight only, while intermediate stations serving small communities on main lines should close, with the aim of speeding up inter-city trains. A total of 2363 stations and halts were to be closed, including 435 under consideration before the report appeared, of which 235 had already been closed.

The proposed mass changes to the network would be implemented in a seven-year programme, the report recommended.

Basically, the report said that railways should be used to meet that part of the national transport requirement for which they offered the best available means, and stop trying to compete in areas where they were now ill-suited.

The report followed a key study initiated by Beeching into traffic flows on all the railway routes in the country.

This study, which had been carried out during the week ending 23 April 1962, two weeks after Easter, found that 30 per cent of route miles carried just one per cent of passengers and freight, and half of all stations contributed just two per cent of income. Half the total route mileage carried about four per cent of the total passenger miles, and around five per cent of the freight ton miles, revenue from them amounting to £20-million with the costs double that figure. Clearly, the figures did not stack up, nor, it seemed, were ever likely to again.

From the least-used half of the stations the gross revenue from all traffic did not even cover the cost of the stations themselves, and made no contribution to route costs, movement or terminal costs.

Regarding branch lines, figures showed it was doubtful if the revenue from up to 6000 passengers a week covered movement costs alone, and clearly money would be saved by withdrawing the service.

The report stated that overall, pas-

senger traffic on a single-track branch line added around £1750 a mile to the cost of route maintenance, signalling and the staffing of stations.

Therefore, a passenger density below 10,000 could not be considered as economic, even where freight traffic absorbed a proportion of the route cost.

Where there was no other traffic, 17,000 passengers per week might make a branch line pay its way.

Even the provision of railbuses – a cost-cutting measure introduced on many branches in the late fifties as a key element of a drive to prune staffing levels and increase efficiency – demanded a passenger density of 14,000 a week, as against 17,000 a week with diesel multiple units.

Beeching stated in the opening to his report that "there had never before been any systematic assembly of a basis of information upon which planning could be founded, and without which the proper role of the railways in the transport system as a whole could not be determined."

Taken at face value, that claimed it was the first time that a detailed study of the economy of the nation's railways as a whole had been attempted, rather than the individual regions of British Railways (Western, London Midland, Eastern, Southern and Scottish) largely doing their own thing. Maybe if such a nationwide study had been attempted

of eliminating non-remunerative lines had been underway for decades. Indeed, several of the routes listed in The Reshaping of British Railways had already been proposed for closure by their regions: Beeching merely confirmed those decisions.

The closures of poorly-used lines had fallen from

350 in 1959 to 175 in 1960, and even further to 150 in 1961. Yet in 1962, the year before The Reshaping of British Railways appeared, they shot up to 780. The Western Region, for one, which had embraced dieselisation, was making much publicity out of the improvements it was making, after years of closing branches serving rural backwaters.

In 1963, before the newly-recommended Beeching closures could be implemented, 324 miles were axed.

By taking a global view and applying the same criteria to all regions across the country, Beeching may be seen as merely streamlining the decision-making processes that had gone before, with a universal set of criteria. Not only that, it was Marples who employed him and instructed him – the doctor was "only obeying orders."

Much of the report proposed that

as part of the implementation of the Modernisation Plan, it would not have been implemented in such a haphazard, localised and floundering manner.

The report read: "Throughout these investigations and the preparation of this report the British Railways Board has had it in mind that its duty is to employ the assets vested in it, and develop or modify them, to the best advantage of the nation."

As we have seen, Beeching did not invent rail closures: a steady process

ABOVE Collett auto tank No 1453 and trailer W244W moves off from Sharpness with the 4.15pm service to Berkeley road on 26 September 1964. The Sharpness branch closed to passengers in November 1964 and goods in January 1966, but the line serving Sharpness Docks was retained, and is now being revived by enthusiasts as the Berkeley Vale Railway

British Rail electrify some trunk routes and eliminate uneconomic wagon-load traffic in favour of containerised freight traffic.

The report – which claimed that the measures should eradicate the railways' deficit by 1970 – automatically sparked immediate outrage from many of the communities which would become disenfranchised by the rail network as a result of the closures.

However, the Conservative Government, which accepted Beeching's report after it was debated in the House of Commons in April 1963, promised that axed rail services would be replaced by bus services, which would be much cheaper to operate.

The report said: "Today, rail stopping services and bus services serve the same basic purpose. Buses carry the greater part of the passengers moving by public transport in rural areas, and, as well as competing with each other, both forms of public transport are fighting a losing battle against private transport.

"Immediately prior to the war, in 1938, the number of private cars registered was 1,944,000. In 1954 there were 3,100,000, and in 1961 there were 6,000,000. By 1970 it is expected that there will be a total of 13,000,000 cars registered, equivalent to 24.3 per 100 of the population or 76 per 100 families."

Looking back, major flaws in the report may be seen as a failure to

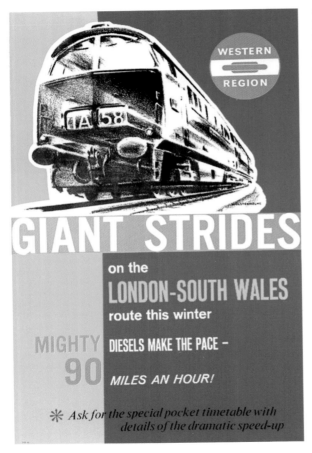

consider neither reduction of costs on lossmaking services and electrification to countermand competition from road alternatives. Neither were subsidies considered or asked for, as Beeching intended that his slimline railway network would eliminate its deficit within a few years.

When the report was debated by both the Commons and the country, it was in the year leading up to a General Election. It might therefore seem surprising that such unpopular measures were introduced before an election rather than after it.

Yet while the Labour opposition led by Harold Wilson said it would reverse the Beeching cuts if elected, the Conservatives steamed ahead with the report's implementation.

There appeared to be a general feeling that once protestors had been given their chance to vent their anger through initial newspaper headlines, there would be a growing general acceptance that closures were inevitable.

Marples approved the vast majority of closures which reached him for consideration, although the consultative machinery conveniently held back the first impact of the programme until the

Beeching's 15-point tonic

The Reshaping of British Railways identified 15 steps which needed to be taken to bring about the turnaround in fortunes envisaged by Beeching. These were:

1. The discontinuation of many stopping passenger services.

2. The transfer of the modern diesel multiple-unit stock displaced to continuing services which are still steam hauled.

3. The closure of a large number of small stations to passenger traffic, eliminating loss-making stops which slowed down trains.

4. Improvement to inter-city passenger services and rationalisation of routes.

5. The damping down of seasonal peaks of passenger traffics and withdrawal of corridor coaching stock held to cover them. In particular, this bode ill for branch lines serving holiday resorts, such as those on the London & South

LEFT A single green railcar in station waits at the GWR's Bromyard station, although there were far more weeds than passengers by then, it closed on 7 September 1969

FAR LEFT 'Giant Strides' is an A N Wolstenholme poster produced for British Railways to promote improvements in the speed of trains on the London-South Wales route with the introduction of diesels that travelled at 90mph

election campaign was well underway.

The few he spared from the axe included important electrified commuter routes such as Manchester to Bury and Liverpool to Southport.

In February 1964, Marples made one concession – promising to close no seaside branch lines before October that year, so people could plan their holidays for the coming summer.

Western Railway's 'Withered Arm' system in Devon and Cornwall, where traffic levels boomed during the peak summer season but services were little used by locals during the rest of the year. The annual cost of providing the 6000 coaches for the summer season was £3.4-million, set against total revenue of just £500,000.

6. The co-ordination of suburban train and bus services and charges.

7. The co-ordination of passenger parcels service with the Post Office.

8. An increase in block train movements of coal by inducing the National Coal Board to provide train-loading facilities at collieries and the provision of coal concentration depots.

9. The reduction of uneconomic freight

traffic by closing small goods stations and the adjustment of charges, in other words, the end of the traditional pick-up goods, with road hauliers ready and willing to fill the void.

10. The attraction of more sidings-to-sidings traffic by the operation of through trains at the expense of the system of forwarding of single wagons.

11. The study and development of the "liner" train system.

12. The concentration of the freight sundries traffic on 100 main depots.

13. The rapid and progressive withdrawal of freight wagons over the following three years.

14. The continued replacement of steam by diesel traction for main line services up to a probable requirement of at least 3750 to 4250 locomotives. At the time of the report, 1698 diesels were already in service and 950 on order.

15. The rationalisation of the composition and use of the railways' road cartage fleet.

LEFT The Hayling Island branch was closed by Beeching on 3 November 1963 even though it made a small profit. British Railways gave the reason as the cost of replacing the timber swing bridge which crossed Langstone Harbour comprised an unreasonably large investment

Chapter 5

The backlash and backpedalling

Back in 1935, when a protest meeting was held in a bid to stop the Southern Railway from closing the Lynton & Barnstaple Railway, a telling question killed the debate, like a pin bursting a balloon. The packed room was asked how many attendees had travelled by the railway that day. The lack of raised hands spoke volumes.

Many railway lines that closed in the 50s died a death with hardly a murmur. Others were marked by special enthusiasts' trains to mark the last day.

When there were local opposition groups, it was too often a case of people who might have used the railway protesting too much about the fact it would soon no longer be an option. Joni Mitchell said "you don't know what you've got til it's gone" and in so many cases that applied to branch lines. In many cases, people saw the closure notices as foregone conclusions.

However, the sheer scale of the Beeching cuts, coming on top of 780 miles closed in 1962 and another 324 in 1964, led to nationwide rather than localised anger, from rail users, local residents, civic representatives and the unions.

Protest marches were held, councils voted against closure, MPs were lobbied, accounts were disseminated to provide fresh arguments that certain lines could be made viable, but in most cases to no avail. In fairness, not every proposed closure or withdrawal of service listed in Beeching's 1963 report was carried through, but there were many other cases where local people felt that

they had done enough in presenting counter arguments, only to be left with the feeling that they fell on deaf ears and had been left standing in the path of an unstoppable steamroller left on autopilot.

Lord Stonham, the Labour peer who had been the only member of the party ever to be elected MP for Taunton, and later won the inner London seat of Shoreditch and Finsbury, launched a broadside against the Beeching report and its backers in a speech to the House of Lords on 2 May 1963.

Beginning by mentioning the Minister of Transport's statement that 25,726 jobs would disappear, he said: "...the whole difficulty, the whole acute public anxiety which undoubtedly exists throughout the country about the Beeching Plan is, in my view, attributable to what the noble Viscount (Lord Hailsham) called Mr Marples' flair for publicity: the terrific public relations job which has been done on the presentation of this Plan, and its blowing up out of all reasonable sense of proportion."

Commenting on Ernest Marples' statement to the Commons that the period ending in September 1964 "... will see the most intensive implementation of the plan on the assumption that closures will go as fast as anyone could reasonably expect." Lord Stonham said: "The precise mention of the number of jobs which are going to be lost indicates that the decision, in so far as it can

LEFT On the Isle of Wight, Beeching wanted to close everything apart from the Ryde Pier section, which would take ferry passengers from one end of the pier to the other. Local campaigners forced a compromise with Ryde-Shanklin remaining open. Why the entire line could not have been saved through to Ventnor remains a permanent subject for debate. Steam trains were withdrawn from Ryde Pier on 17 September, and the whole line on 31 December 1966, after which it was converted to allow 750V third-rail electrification to take place. At the same time, it was decided to increase the height of the trackbed in Esplanade Tunnel, to reduce flooding by very high tides and the need to pump out seawater afterwards. The diminished clearance would no longer allow trains built to the national loading gauge to run beneath it, so rolling stock built to a lower height was required. Second-hand London Underground tube trains provided the answer and are still running there today

be made, has already been made; and almost every word that the Minister of Transport says on this subject is proof positive that the minds of the Government have been made up."

He raised the issue of the planned closure of rail connections to Stranraer, the ferry port for Northern Ireland, asking Lord Hailsham if he was "aware that 40 per cent of the people who go on the boat to Larne in Northern Ireland go by rail to Stranraer; that the steamer's income increased to £286,000 this year from £200,000 the year before, and that Ayrshire County Council are afraid that if the rail link is broken they will eventually lose the steamer and the short sea route to Ireland altogether?"

He described Marples' promised consultation on the Stranraer line as "the kind of consultation that a condemned man gets when they ask him what he wants for breakfast before they hang him."

Lord Stonham said: "Many of the figures in the Beeching Report are known to be wrong, although unfortunately none of them can be really checked."

He said that many of its provisions – the reduction in stopping and branch line services; closure of little-used wayside stations or their conversion to halts; reductions in passenger stock and wagons; great reduction in the number of marshalling yards, plus resiting and modernising; larger wagons, particularly for mineral traffic; complete reorientation of freight services to speed movement and reduce costs and provide direct transits for main streams of traffic and attract to the railway a due proportion of the full load merchandise traffic which would otherwise pass by road – had been spelled out in the British Railways 1955 Modernisation Plan. This was "faithfully copied" into the Beeching report – despite Marples' statement that there has been nothing like it before in the history of British Railways.

He said that unlike the Modernisation Plan eight year earlier, it had "occasioned anger – anger cutting across party barriers; anger deeper and more widespread, in my opinion, throughout the country than almost any domestic issue during the last 20 years."

He asked why the only pleasant comment he had heard on the plan "is the advice to use Dr Beeching's face cream because it removes all lines."

He suggested that while the 1955 plan had been announced as being "not designed merely to make our railway system self-supporting: it aims at producing far-reaching benefits for the economy of the country as a whole and for the better ordering of its transport arrangements."

Beeching was not allowed to spare a thought for the economy of the country as a whole.

Also, whereas the Modernisation Plan aimed to benefit the whole country, including the parts furthest away from the main industrial centres like Scotland, Wales and the west of England, all of those areas would "have virtually ceased to exist" under the Beeching proposals.

Lord Stonham added: "In 1955 the same ideas were presented with wisdom as a means of rehabilitation, re-equipment and, in some cases, expansion. In 1963 it has been brutal surgery allied to mishandling so foolish as to appear deliberate."

Crucially, he shifted the blame from the man whose name appeared on the report, and which has become synonymous with rail closures. He continued: "For this

I blame the Government; certainly not Dr Beeching, Indeed, one can only blame such an outstanding technologist for having accepted his task with such limited terms of reference and thus inevitably producing an intellectual exercise in a vacuum; as any plan for the railways must be when it is conducted in isolation from other forms of transport and from the economic and social needs of the country."

LEFT LNER V2 2-6-2 No 60836 stands inside the impressive North Eastern Railway terminus at Alnwick waiting to work the 5.55pm to Alnmouth on I June 1966. The station was closed in 1968, but the trainshed remains intact and in use as a bookshop for Barter Books. The Aln Valley Railway is planning to rebuild as much of this three-mile line as possible

A penny a week 'would stave off closures'

Lord Stonham called, in vain as it turned out, for a postponement on closures until it was known what they would cost the country, and the longer-term, fundamental question of the national cost relationship between road and rail was answered. He pointed out that in recent years, 340 branch lines and 4000 miles of track had been closed – saving the railways less than one per cent, or two old pence in the pound of their total costs. He said that the expected saving of £18-million a year by closing 5000 miles of passenger services was equivalent to just four days' defence expenditure. "Compare £18-million with the £2350-million allowed on tax-free expenses – most of it on tax-free cars," he said. "Would an £180-million branch line subsidy be a worse way of spending money than the much larger business car subsidy? "This sum of £18-million a year means one penny a week for each one of us.

He also drew attention to the high summer patronage of closure-ear-marked branch lines, when some of the doomed stations received 100 times their daily winter average of passengers, and predicted that the already-choked roads would have to shoulder this burden during holiday times if the closures went ahead.

He also questioned Marples' statement that if the railways attracted all the traffic they want from the roads after the implementation of the Beeching report, road traffic would fall by two per cent. While the Beeching report proposed to cut 900 freight depots down to 100 larger ones, extra lorries would be needed, and they would all be in congested areas.

Lord Stonham criticised the Minister for not having plans in place to widen and improve roads to handle the extra traffic before closing branch lines.

He said: "The closure of the marginal Peterborough-Grimsby line will isolate a large part of Lincolnshire, including towns like Skegness, which will be 23 miles from the nearest railway station. The roads are comparatively narrow and wind extraordinarily, and 150 miles will need straightening and widening. At £100,000 a mile, that means £15-million for only one area.

"In addition, it will put an enormous burden on ratepayers at the very time when they are losing income because people will not be going to the seaside resorts. How much it is going to cost on immediate works the Minister does not know. My guess is that it well may be £1000-million, and as the estimates come in, that may well prove to be an underestimate. This cost alone is going to knock the £18-million a year silly. How can the closure procedure be started before this information is available?

"There are literally scores of what I regard as utterly daft proposals in this Plan. In the Rhondda, there is a

two-mile railway tunnel under the mountains. It is proposed to continue the railway for freight but not for passengers. To get to the other side of

the mountain by road entails travelling 40 miles and the roads round are not suitable for buses.

"Out of 195,000 miles of highways, there will be thousands of miles which will need major and costly improvements if they are to carry buses and lorries safely."

Lord Stonham described as "utter nonsense" the Commons statement by

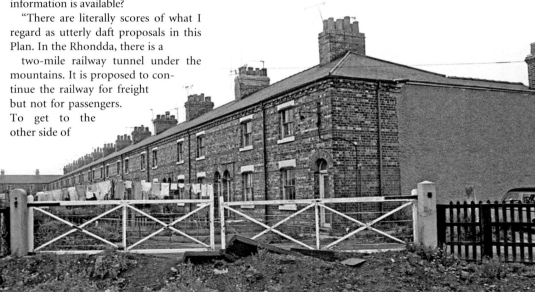

BELOW Great Northern Railway-built eight-road Colwick shed (38A) at Nottingham closed on Sunday 4 April 1965. The locality had acquired a sense of dereliction and despair by August 1971

Marples that 100 extra buses would cover the 15,000 square miles of Scotland left entirely without railways.

"What sort of confidence does it inspire when he tells the doomed areas not to worry because he personally will have to approve every closure?" he said. "That is precisely what does worry them."

In the days before Lord Stonham's speech, a resolution passed by the National Council on Inland Transport at a conference which included representatives of 170 local authorities from all parts of Britain passed a resolution which stated that it was "appalled by the social and economic consequences of Dr Beeching's Report and demands that it shall not be implemented until all the consequences and costs to the nation have been fully assessed."

The country in uproar

The County Councils Association of England and every major authority in Scotland, Wales and the west of England followed up the resolution with similar demands.

Lord Stonham said: "This adds up to a unanimous and overwhelming

demand from non-party organisations representing virtually the entire population. Any minister, in my view, would have to be either mentally subnormal or morally delinquent to ignore this overwhelming demand and the local knowledge and facts on which it is based."

Regarding public subsidies to railways, Lord Stonham accused the Government of merely switching them to roads, so haulage "can profitably quote freight rates which put the railways out of business. That is the economics of Bedlam."

He said that taking into account road construction and maintenance which was rising to £250-million a year, the £230-million annual cost of accidents, £130-million spent on police signals and traffic control, the Road Federation's estimated cost of congestion placed at £500-million a year and damage to buildings at £100-million a year gave a total of £1210-million a year. With fuel duties and vehicle taxes brought in around half this sum, it revealed a net subsidy to road transport of over £600-million a year – four times the railway deficit.

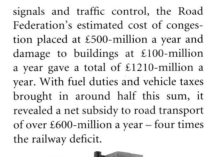

RIGHT 'Black Five'
4-6-0 No 45113 at
Northampton Castle
on 2 May 1964,
the last day of services,
after which the route
to Peterborough
closed to passengers

"In other words, the roads are a far bigger national loss maker that the railways," he added.

Nonetheless, Lord Stonham said that he still saw "much to commend" in the Beeching report, particularly with the proposals to boost freight. "But they cannot succeed unless we see to it that they get the chance to compete (with road haulage) on equal terms," he said.

"We should ask Dr Beeching to look again, not at how easily he can close lines down, but at what must be done to keep them open.

"Give them a facelift: apply with goodwill the many methods whereby costs can be lowered by running modified services, rather than destroy them altogether.

"Use and foster the growing interest of many local authorities in their railway and their anxiety to increase its business.

"Jettison the idea, which our people will never accept, that they must holiday abroad because British Railways will make no provision for holidays in Britain.

"Before the war, students used to come from all over the world to watch and learn from British Railways. They will begin to come again if we call a truce to amputation, and, by infusing modern efficiency with the old spirit of public service, restore our railways to their former position as the envy of the world."

While several of the lines he mentioned were eventually spared the axe, and Skegness for one is still served by rail, most of his counter arguments against the Beeching closures fell on deaf ears.

History was left to judge how many of them were valid, balanced by the fact that despite Marples' personal interest in roads, the switch from rail to road and the growth in car ownership at the expense of railway branch lines was a global phenomenon by no means restricted to Britain.

By the time Labour replaced the Tories in office in late 1964, "Beeching Must Go" was almost a national war cry.

To add balance to Lord Stonham's criticisms of the Beeching report, it should be remembered that while it was a Conservative government that called for the network to be rationalised, it was to be the ensuing Labour government, a party long associated with verbal support for public transport, and which before it won the General Elections in 1964 pledged to reverse the Beeching cuts, that nonetheless implemented most of it. Lord Stonham went on to serve as a Home Office junior minister from 1964-67 in Harold Wilson's Labour government and as Minister of State in the Home Office with responsibility for Northern Ireland until 1969, when he was appointed as a privy counsellor.

An expert's view

The Great Central Association, a corporate member of the National Council on Inland Transport, published a report by Professor ER Hondelink, MSc, MICE, MInstT, which argued that had Britain's roads been subjected to a Beeching-style study, the case for closing railways en masse would have quickly fallen through.

Prof Hondelink, a consultant to the United Nations Technical Assistance Service, said: "Dr Beeching's pronouncement that there is no sensible alternative to his plan must be challenged with the greatest vigour."

He said that the one-sided Government approach had ignored "the identical but more complicated and more serious problem of overall economic road transport deficits" and outlined the position as he saw it as follows:

"Roads provided, owned, maintained, administered and paid for by 1288 highway authorities, used by millions of transporters, individuals, groups and companies. Accounts legion in numbers, complicated and not easily analysed. Widespread research in other lands compared with position here point to the likelihood that overall deficit – ultimately born by taxpayer and ratepayer – is far in excess of the railway deficit. It is certainly at least £300-million, may well be as high as £600-million.

"If a similar exercise were carried out on the roads and road transport sector, it is probable that the bottom would fall out of Dr Beeching's report."

The professor, who had just stood down as Director General of the European Central Inland Transport Organisation, and who clearly "knew his stuff", said that many rail routes had been subjected to "calculated neglect and starvation" prior to closure, and that the additional burden on the highway authorities of transferring rail traffic to roads had been ignored.

As did many critics of Beeching, he stressed the importance of loss-making branch lines as feeders of traffic to the main line, and said other countries that had closed unremunerative branch lines had later reopened them.

He urged, largely in vain at it happened, the Government to order the British Railways Board to probe road and other transport costs in the same way Beeching had addressed the railways, to postpone all closures until such studies had been completed and to immediately concentrate on making maximum and more economic use of existing equipment, while reducing staff by operational and administrative methods already in widespread use on continental Europe.

Labour's broken promise

Under Harold Wilson's Labour government elected in 1964, the pre-election promise to halt the Beeching closures was not only quickly and conveniently forgotten, but also the closures continued at a faster rate than under Marples.

In 1964, the first year that many of the Beeching recommendations took effect, 1058 miles were closed, followed by 600 in 1965, in the first year of the Wilson administration.

In December 1965, The Railway Magazine correspondent Onlooker, in pleading for a square deal for the railways after what he called a "year of frustration", commented: "The Reshaping report listed 267 passenger services to be withdrawn and 2363 stations and halts to be closed. Over 300 parliamen-

tary constituencies were affected, yet not a single Tory MP voted against its approval.

"Also, since changing sides in the House, not a single Labour MP has had the courage to remind the party's leaders about this unredeemed pledge.

"Back in their constituencies, however, they bay to a different moon. Whenever a public inquiry is held by the Transport Users' Consultative Committee into a proposed withdrawal of a service, local MPs, whether Tory or Labour, line up to lead the objectors.

ABOVE With the famous abbey on the right of the horizon, the 12.50pm Middlesbrough-Scarborough diesel multiple unit service enters Whitby on 6 March 1965, the last day of passenger services between there and Scarborough. Harold Wilson forgot his pre-election pledge to specifically save this route

BRITISH RAILWAYS BOARD (M)

BR 4405

LLANFAIRPWLLGWYNGYLLGOGERYCHWYRNDROBWLLLLANTYSILIOGOGOGOCH

F 50856

50856

PLATFORM TICKET 3d.

**AVAILABLE ONE HOUR ON DAY OF ISSUE ONLY
NOT VALID IN TRAINS, NOT TRANSFERABLE.**

FOR CONDITIONS SEE OVER

| 1 | 2 | 3 | 4 | 5 | 6 | 7 | 8 | 9 | 10 | 11 | 12 |

ABOVE The fact that sentimentality for railways did not even come bottom of the list of priorities, but did not feature at all in the Beeching report of 1963 is highlighted by the fact that the famous station at Llanfairpwllgwyngyllgogerychwyrndrobwllllantysiliogogogoch on the Bangor-Holyhead line was axed in 1966 along with most other stopping stations on the route in a bid to speed up journey times between primary destinations.

As Hamlet might have said: 'Thus a three-line whip does make cowards of us all... and enterprises of great pith and moment, with this regard, their currents turn away and lose the name of action.'

"The root cause of Labour's betrayal of rail is not far to seek. There are 2,500,000 workers employed in the road transport industry, while the BR payroll barely reaches 500,000 – a ratio of 5 to 1. Can a Government deal fairly with a plaintiff's case when there are five bellicose defendants breathing down its neck?"

In 1966, another 750 miles were closed, followed by 300 miles in 1967, 400 in 1968, 250 in 1969 and 275 in 1970. Only then did the rate of closures rapidly fall off.

So while it is easy to shift the blame for the axe on Ernest Marples, the road building minister who appointed Beeching and rubber stamped many of the closures he recommended, it was the Labour opposition that despite its public vows to reverse the trend, stuck to much the same policy once elected, when it also found that it had to make the same hard decisions based on available criteria in the face of the soaring British Railways deficit which accompanied the growth in car ownership.

A seaside resort hit particularly hard was Whitby, where the closure of all three routes to the town was recommended. Local people widely expected the main route to York to be saved; however, in September 1964, just a month before the General Election, Marples surprised everybody by confirming the closure of both the York and Scarborough routes but reprieving the line to Middlesbrough via the Esk Valley.

It was certainly an unusual choice. While the wonderfully scenic Esk Valley route serves several isolated villages, it was far from being the most direct link between Whitby and the main population of Yorkshire. Marples made his decision based on the importance of Whitby itself of retaining a rail service to connect it with the nearest large centre of population, the importance of the tourist trade to the port and the surrounding area and the extreme difficulty of operating buses over the Esk Valley roads, especially in winter.

As part of his campaign, the Labour candidate for Scarborough and Whitby produced a pledge signed by Harold Wilson himself that the remaining closures would not go ahead if his party won the election.

Within a month, Wilson was in Downing Street, ending more than 13 years of Conservative control, but had only a majority of four seats, and it was clear that Wilson would need to go to the polls again sooner rather than later to obtain a comfortable working majority.

How much the Beeching closures played in the downfall of the Conservative Government as opposed to, say, the Profumo scandal and the general mood of modernisation and a desire for change, drawing a line under the 'old order' once and for all, could not be calculated. Yet it was by no means a landslide in favour of those who pledged to stop the Beeching cuts; indeed, apart from the pledge, the closures barely featured in the election campaign.

Looked upon to redeem Labour's pre-election pledge with regard to Whitby, new Transport Minister Tom Fraser claimed that due to a technicality in the 1962 Transport Act, he was powerless to reverse his predecessor Marples' decisions, despite the fact that they had not yet been implemented. Neither did Wilson appear inclined to intervene with a state-controlled industry. The word 'cop-out' comes quickly to mind, and instinctively begs the question – why does the electorate still heed election promises?

Yet there was no widespread uproar over the apparent U-turn. Maybe it was an indication that the new car-owning classes no longer had a reason to care about railways when they had discovered the new liberty that the open road gave them.

Also, many sections of the press were in support of Beeching's attempts to reduce the burden on the taxpayer by ridding the country of sizeable parts of a transport system which was by natural forces of supply and demand becoming obsolete. Indeed, The Railway Magazine had carried an editorial in its May 1963 issue which began: "Whether one agrees with all of 'the plan' or not it has, to be admitted that Dr Beeching's Report is basically correct and backed by such a weight of carefully prepared evidence as to be almost unassailable. It has been described as brutal, brilliant and right."

After turning his back on the promises to Whitby, Fraser authorised 39 out of 40 outstanding closures across the country. It appeared to be nothing less than a case of a seamless join with the Marples administration.

To many, this 'carry on as before' approach underlined the fact that some form of large-scale closure policy was viewed as inescapable on both sides of the political fence in a rapidly changing and modernising world. Therefore from this point of view at least, it is surely unfair or wrong to blame one or two individuals, Marples and Beeching, who found themselves in the time and place where circumstances dictated that they had to grasp the nettle in the first place.

The question is – could the problems of declining demand for rail services and the soaring deficit combined with streamlining the network to ensure its survival have been approached in a different way than that outlined in the Beeching report, and if so, would more or less closures have taken place? Could overall losses have been stemmed or reduced to an acceptable level, maybe by pruning operating costs to bare bones and running lines on a skeletal basis, or would it have been a case of sticking a finger in the dyke and putting off the evil day when far more drastic cutting back would have been inescapable?

A thermometer in the west

One stretch of British road became immortalised by traffic jams in the mid-20th century, firstly as car ownership and leisure time boomed, and secondly, as more car journeys were needed to replace closed railway branch lines to holiday resorts. The Exeter bypass.

The West Country has always been Britain's choice destination for summer holidays, and Exeter was a hub both for journey by rail, with the Great Western and Southern rail lines from London meeting there, along with several of the main roads to both Devon and Cornwall.

By the 1920s, with the new car-owning middle class taking motoring holidays in the west, as opposed to travelling there by train, the city's streets were becoming overburdened, and several buildings had to be demolished for road widening and traffic lights first appeared in 1929. It was suggested that a new road should be built to take passing traffic around the town rather than through it.

Work began on an eastern bypass in the early 1930s, and the first section, from Bath Road west of Pinhoe to the

COUNTY OF DEVON

EXETER BY-PASS

THIS TABLET IS ERECTED TO COMMEMORATE THE OFFICIAL OPENING OF THE EXETER BY-PASS ROAD BY THE RIGHT HON. LESLIE BURGIN, M.P. MINISTER OF TRANSPORT, ON THE 22nd. DAY OF FEBRUARY 1938

ABOVE The plaque marking the opening of the Exeter bypass

Countess Wear roundabout, was completed by 1935. The section included the building of Gallows Bridge at Gallows Cross across the A30 London Road, with a slip road to allow traffic from London to join the bypass, and a roundabout where it crossed the road to Sidmouth at Middlemoor. Gallows Bridge was built from local red sandstone, and to the untrained eye, ironically looks every bit like a railway overbridge. Incidentally, the 'Gallows' recalled the place of execution at Heavitree where three Bideford women were hanged in 1682, when they became the last people

ABOVE Gallows Bridge: you could be forgiven for thinking that it carries a railway rather than the Exeter bypass

in Britain to be documented as being executed for witchcraft.

In August 1935, the building of the final section of the bypass between Countess Wear, running across the River Exe and Exeter Ship Canal to join the roads to Dawlish Road, Torquay and Plymouth began. It included a new swing bridge over the canal specially to accommodate the huge volumes of holiday traffic. This final section was opened by Transport Minister Leslie Burgin on 22 February 1938. The Minister said: "The people of Exeter need have no fear of the bypass for it is better to have willing customers

who can reach the city than disgruntled tourists who are delayed on their journeys through being unable to pass through it."

However, the bypass generated more disgruntled tourists than ever before by the mid-50s, well before the great swathe of branch line closures began. Holiday specials still ran to the West Country resorts behind Great Western King 4-6-0s, but the motor car was rapidly seizing their crown, and queues on the bypass tailed back for hours at peak periods because it was not big enough to cope with the volume. Queues returned big time to Exeter city centre, as frustrated

12-mile tailbacks on the Exeter bypass. By the summer of 1966 they were regularly making national news, as nearby the last rites were being read over branch line services. This situation, while individually notorious in terms of traffic congestion, may be viewed as a microcosm of the changing traffic patterns brought about by the great shift from rail to road, promoted by public demand and perpetuated by government transport policy.

The solution? Build more roads. In 1968, plans to extend the M5 south from Bristol to Exeter, bypassing the bypass, were announced. It was completed in October 1975, and included a new bridge built by British Rail for the surviving branch line to Exmouth.

motorists tried to avoid the bypass. In a bid to address the problems in the summer of 1959, a raised platform was built in the centre of the Countess Wear roundabout, from which a policeman could manually control four sets of temporary traffic lights.

By the mid-60s, rising car ownership combined with more resorts disenfranchised from the rail network saw

The section of the bypass between the Countess Wear roundabout and Dawlish Road still generated traffic queues, at rush hour.

Slow Train

In 1963, the comic songwriting duo Michael Flanders and Donald Swann captured the mood of Britain with a song, Slow Train, about the Beeching cuts. Mentioning many stations including Trouble House Halt, later taken up by other artists including the King's Singers. *It ran as follows:*

Miller's Dale for Tideswell ...
Kirby Muxloe ...
Mow Cop and Scholar Green ...

No more will I go to Blandford Forum
and Mortehoe,
On the slow train from Midsomer
Norton and Mumby Road.
No churns, no porter, no cat on a seat
At Chorlton-cum-Hardy or Chester-le-Street.
We won't be meeting again
On the Slow Train.

I'll travel no more from Littleton Badsey
to Openshaw.
At Long Stanton I'll stand well clear of the doors
no more.
No whitewashed pebbles, no Up and no Down
From Formby Four Crosses to Dunstable Town.
I won't be going again
On the Slow Train.

On the Main Line and the Goods Siding
The grass grows high
At Dog Dyke, Tumby Woodside
And Trouble House Halt.

The Sleepers sleep at Audlem and Ambergate.
No passenger waits on Chittening platform or
Cheslyn Hay.
No one departs, no one arrives
From Selby to Goole, from St Erth to St Ives.
They've all passed out of our lives
On the Slow Train, on the Slow Train.

Cockermouth for Buttermere...
on the Slow Train,
Armley Moor Arram...
Pye Hill and Somercotes...
on the Slow Train,
Windmill End.

Michael Flanders and Donald Swann

Chapter 6

More closures, followed by compassion

On 23 December 1965, Barbara Castle was appointed as Transport Minister. She became famous as the person who introduced the breathalyser to tackle the rising problem of drink-driving, and also made the 70mph motorway speed limit permanent.

She was behind legislation that ruled that that all cars had to be fitted with seat-belts.

Furthermore, she oversaw the closure of around 2050 miles of railway lines both under the Beeching plan along with routes that the doctor had not proscribed, such as Buxton to Matlock, and so her appointment was in that respect far from a U-turn..

However, under her 1968 Transport Act, she importantly introduced a new social factor into legislation regarding such closures, and a further 3500 miles were given the possibility of a reprieve.

While, as we have already seen, the Labour government under Wilson had reneged big time on its 1964 pre-election pledge to halt the Beeching cuts, it had become increasingly apparent that not only had the rail closures not produced anything like the promised savings or ended the British Railways deficit but were unlikely ever to do so.

Castle recognised that while many services earmarked for closure were unremunerative, they nonetheless played a vital social role, and if they closed, the communities they served would suffer hardship.

Her first role in the government had

been as the first Minister for Overseas Development, and she was only the fourth woman in history ever to hold position in a British cabinet.

She had hoped to win a bigger seat in the Cabinet, and at first did not want the transport portfolio (she could not even drive) but Wilson told her that he needed a 'tiger in the tank' in that department, quoting the Esso petrol advertising slogan of the day.

However, once appointed, she quickly warmed to the challenge. By 1966, the year when the Exeter bypass was making even bigger summer headlines than ever before, roads were carrying 90 per cent of passenger mileage and 60 per cent of freight ton mileage. However, the laws regarding road safety had not caught up with the great switch from rail, while urban areas were creaking under the weight of the upsurge in traffic.

That year, 8000 people died on the roads. "One for the road" drivers could drink as much as they liked and drive as fast as they liked.

Castle's subsequent 1967 Road Safety Act saved lives. It brought in not only the breathalyser but a year's ban for those who failed it. At the end of the first five months of its use, it was estimated that 800 lives had been saved by it.

Not everyone liked the idea: she was even sent a death threat by an angry motorist. However, while realising that the car was now king and would stay so, she wanted to see a new integrated transport policy that not only accepted that fact but would breathe new life into public transport, particularly in urban areas where congestion was making its mark. That would have to include, as Stanley Raymond had stated following the departure of Beeching, subsidies to commuter lines.

She said: "I refused to be a King Canute trying to force people onto railways which could not take them where they wanted to go.

"If the private car had brought the boon of mobility to millions of people, which it clearly had, then that boon should be available to everyone. We must collectively face the consequences and deal with them through new arrangements which reflected the new facts."

Despite some successes of modernisation such as the Freightliner container trains, British Rail could not make its still-enormous freight system pay its way, when faced with stiffening competition from lorry transport.

Castle tried to introduce balance by having road hauliers soak up more of the expense they imposed on the roads. She also improved road haulage safety standards, by introducing the tachograph which limited drivers' daily hours – a move by which the left-winger aroused deep anger from the trade unions.

A new National Freight Corporation would encompass Freightliner and British Rail's, remaining road freight services to create a streamlined competitive single unit, again provoking the fury of the Transport & General Workers Union.

While railway closures rolled on at a very high rate, she saved several individual routes including branch lines; York to Harrogate, Manchester to Buxton, Oxenholme to Windermere, Exeter to Exmouth and in Cornwall, the Looe branch and the St Ives line.

With regard to the latter two, Barbara Castle called Beeching's plans "slaugh-

holiday traffic on to the roads which couldn't cope with it.

"Nor would extensive and expensive road improvements have been the answer. At St Ives, these would have involved destroying the whole character of the town. At Looe, they could not have avoided long delays in the holiday season.

"It would have been the economics of Bedlam to spend vast sums only to create greater inconvenience."

In a similar vein, part of the Bere-Alston to Callington branch was saved, because of the hilly terrain at the point where the rivers Tamar and Tavy meet and the circuitous road routes. The branch was truncated at Gunnislake, and the Section of the Southern railway's Plymouth-Exeter main line which was lifted in 1968 was retained as far north as Bere Alston. A new station was built at Gunnislake in 1994.

She also spared Hope and Edale stations on the Manchester-Chinley-Sheffield line, which served in the Peak District National Park. However, at the same time, she allowed the closure of the Buxton-Matlock route to passengers: since the early Seventies, revivalists under the banner of Peak Rail have been trying to rebuild it.

ter of the innocents" and described the St Erth to St Ives as the most beautiful coastal journey in the country.

The Looe branch was saved because of the difficult winding roads serving the resort. Mrs Castle said: "In spite of the financial savings to the railways, it just wouldn't have made sense in the wider context to have transferred heavy

LEFT On 21 September 2008, Transport Secretary Ruth Kelly joined the family of Barbara Castle to help name a Northern Rail train after the late Labour MP and first woman Transport Minister, to mark the 40th anniversary of the 1968 Transport Act. Castle's niece Sonya Hinton (pictured left) unveiled her name on the train at the ceremony, organised by the Passenger Transport Executive Group, at Manchester Oxford Road station.

As Minister, Barbara Castle tackled the problem of financing the railways, and wrote off more than a billion pounds of British Rail's debt.

She introduced the means by which both national and regional government would be able to subsidise lossmaking parts of the network that nonetheless provided wider social and economic benefits.

Section 39 of the 1968 Act introduced the first Government subsidies for such lines. Grants could be paid where three conditions were met.

Firstly, the line had to be unremu-

nerative. Secondly, it was desirable for social or economic reasons for the passenger services to continue, and thirdly, it was financially unreasonable to expect British Rail to provide those services without a grant.

The Act saved several branch lines from closure, but some, like the aforementioned Waverley Route and the Barnstaple-Ilfracombe line and, still did not qualify under criteria and were axed as Beeching intended. Indeed, the Varsity Line that linked the university cities of Oxford and Cambridge saw services withdrawn from the Oxford-

FAR LEFT Sixties icon the Midland Pullman waits at Platform 6 at Manchester Central station on 6 October 1965. This service was discontinued with the start of full electric services between Piccadilly and Euston on 15 April 1966.

ABOVE Barbara Castle saved the St Ives branch from closure, and on 27 May 1978 Lelant Saltings station was opened to provide a park and ride facility for visitors to the often-congested resort arriving by car. First Great Western Class 150 diesel multiple unit No 150221 leaving with 1.25pm to St Erth. FGW

Bletchley section and the Bedford-Cambridge section at the end of 1967, even though the line had not been listed for closure in Beeching's 1963 report.

By the time the 1968 Transport Act had been passed, many lines and services and railway lines that would have qualified for subsidies had already been closed, making it a case of shutting the stable door after the horse had bolted.

While this approach was a marked change from the Beeching report of 1963, in fairness the doctor had never

been given a social factor remit of this type, and had been told to make whatever moves he saw fit on a financial basis to eliminate the railways' rapidly-worsening deficit. From that view, it might be considered unfair to criticise Beeching's findings in themselves, as opposed to the implementation of them by Ernest Marples.

Castle's approach to subsiding railways has continued to this day. Yet it was not only railways that were by now suffering financially. The remaining private bus companies, some of which had put the branch lines out of business, were also struggling against rising car ownership. The 1968 Act placed more of the national bus network under the National Bus Company, formed from 1 January 1969, by merging the bus operating companies of the Government-owned Transport Holding Company with those of the privately-owned British Electric Traction Company Limited, a large nationwide conglomerate, while fuel subsidies were increased and a fleet replacement grant introduced. Licensing for mini-buses was eased and a rural bus grant introduced.

For the cities, the Act legislated for integrated public transport networks to be set up: the Greater London Council would take over London Transport and elsewhere, new Passenger Transport Executives would be set up. These would have wide-ranging powers to integrate local road and rail services, running local buses and harmonising with British Rail on commuter fares and services.

The Marples-era weighting towards

road building was eradicated with the capital grant regime adjusted so that public transport as well as roads projects, could benefit from 75 per cent capital grants.

It was not just railways facing route closures in the Sixties. Their predecessors, the canals were also being prepared for mass pruning.

As a point of clarification, it is often assumed that railways killed off the canals. This was certainly true in some cases, but the inland waterway network

ABOVE Passenger services were withdrawn from the GWR Cinderford branch in November 1958, but the town station remained in use as a goods depot until August 1967. In July 1967, a pair of sheep wander on to little Cinderford Bridge Halt long deserted by passengers

lived on alongside the railways until well into the 20th century.

It was the big freeze of 1962/63 which by and large sounded the death knell for large-scale freight traffic on canals, when barges were left frozen into position for several weeks.

In 1967, the Government wanted to close canals to save money, but Barbara Castle managed to stave off the threat. She kept closures on the 1400-mile network to a minimum while reclassifying canals into commercial and leisure categories, recognising that pleasure boating was on the up. She said that her approach promised "new hope for those who love and use our canals, whether for cruising, angling or just walking on the towpath, or who want to see stretches of canal in some of our unlovely built up areas, developed as centres of beauty or fun."

Both the Conservative opposition and trade unions fought hard against the Bill for the 1968 Act, with Enoch Powell even telling the House of Commons that it was 'evil'.

Despite around 2500 amendments and a record 45 committee sittings, Castle refused to water down her proposals, and her stance made her, according to opinion polls, the most popular Minister in Wilson's Government, which for various reasons had by then lost much favour with the public.

Her success as Transport Minister led to her being moved to the role of Minister for Employment before the Bill was completed, but not before British Rail chairman Stanley Raymond was forced to resign in late 1967 following a disagreement with her, and received a settlement of £28,000 as he was contracted to serve until 1970.

It's getting better

Raymond, later Sir Stanley Raymond, was replaced as British Rail chairman by Sir Henry (Bill) Johnson, who had joined the London & North Eastern Railway and rose through the ranks to become general manager of the London Midland Region in 1958 and its chairman in 1963-7. He took charge of the electrification of the Euston to Manchester and Liverpool line, and the development of new Euston station.

Railways finances improved under Johnson, largely as a result of the 1968 Transport Act, in which the government promised grants to prop up loss-making passenger services where they were providing a public service.

InterCity, started in 1966 as a branded operation of high-speed trains linking major cities, expanded, and in 1969, work began at the Derby Research Centre on the Advanced Passenger Train.

He took charge of the commercial development of surplus railway land, which realised £20-million a year for British Railways in the seventies. He made progress towards improving industrial relations and despite the cut-backs which continued under Labour, he was popular with railway staff, many of who saw him as one of their own.

He was appointed CBE in 1962, knighted in 1968, and became KBE in 1972, the year after he stepped down from railways.

LEFT The line to Bude closed on 3 October 1966, also sounding the end for Halwill Junction, where the North Cornwall Railway route to Launceston and Padstow and the line to Torrington diverged. A housing estate stands near the site of the station, on a road named Beeching Close.

FAR LEFT The twin East Devon branches to Sidmouth and Budleigh Salterton lost their passenger services on 6 March 1967

Chapter 7

The end of mass closures

By the early seventies, the map of the British Rail network looked very much as it does today. In 1970, 275 miles were closed, followed by 23 in 1971, 50 in 1972, 35 in 1973 and none in 1974.

By then, all the blatant lossmakers for which there were no social arguments to keep open had gone, and it was becoming increasingly clear that closures were having a negative impact.

The small amount of money saved by closing a line was outweighed by the increasing road congestion and pollution from motor vehicle exhausts.

One shock closure on 5 January 1970 which stood out from the rest was that of the 1500V DC electrified Woodhead Route between Sheffield and Manchester. The electrification had been completed in 1955 when the upgraded line was opened amid a blaze of publicity.

Its controversial closure just 15 years later, and for which Beeching was not responsible, came after it was decided that the alternative Hope Valley line through Edale would be to stay open instead, for social and network reasons, and would accommodate all Manchester-Sheffield passenger traffic. The Woodhead Route's Class 77 locomotives for passenger traffic were sold to the Netherlands Railways.

The line remained open for freight, mainly coal trains from Yorkshire to Fiddlers Ferry power station near Widnes which required a switch to diesel haulage for the final stage. However, a downturn in coal trade and a need to replace the ageing Class 76 locomotives led to the trans-Pennine route's closure east of Hadfield, with the last train running on 17 July 1981. Hopes of reopening the line quickly ended when most of the line east of Hadfield was lifted in the mid-1980s, but there are still regular calls for the powers that be to second thoughts, despite the conversion of part of the trackbed to a cyclepath.

In October 1973, members of Organization of Arab Petroleum Exporting Countries declared an oil embargo in response to the decision of the USA to resupply the Israeli army during the Yom Kippur war.

Provoking fuel shortages in Britain, just as the 2011 Libyan crisis has seen the price of fuel at the pumps soar, the embargo lasted until March 1974, but by then had showed that it was folly to rely on road transport alone, and what was needed was an energy efficient and adequate public transport network.

One of the last Beeching closures was the GWR branch from Maiden Newton on the main line to Weymouth to Bridport.

BELOW BR's last full set of maroon coaches had a regular Saturdays-only outing on a Derby – Skegness working during the summer of 1974. Class 25s Nos 25126 and 25127 arrive at Boston on 31 August 1974

Initially closure had been staved off because the narrow roads of the locality prompted a subsidy from Dorset County Council. However, the final trains ran in May 1975.

In the north of England, the Haltwhistle-Alston branch in the Pennines had survived Beeching's closure recommendation because of the lack of an all-weather road as an alternative. It lingered on until 3 May 1976 with the last train running two days earlier.

By the mid-seventies, with the last of the Beeching closure out of the way, the network had shrunk to 12,000 miles of track and 2000 stations, around the same size it is now.

One Beeching closure was not enacted until 1985. It was the line from Eridge to Tunbridge Wells, which had been earmarked for the axe along with services from Brighton to Tonbridge.

Tunbridge Wells West station was itself listed for closure in 1966, but subsequently reprieved. However, services on the line were restricted to shuttles between Tonbridge and Eridge with a few through trains to Uckfield.

By the early 1980s the track and signalling needed to be replaced. British Rail decided that the cost of keeping the line from Eridge to Tunbridge Wells Central station open by Grove Junction did not justify the cost of £175,000. Despite public objections, the line closed from 6 July 1985. It was believed though that Tunbridge Wells West station was the last on British Rail to have gas lighting.

A serpent from Serpell

Apart from the years 1978-80, when passenger numbers grew in successive years, the overall decline which had begun in 1957 continued.

Rock bottom was reached in 1982 with the lowest number of passenger journeys of the second half of the 20th century, possibly as a result of a rail strike over rostering arrangements, the lowest level of passenger miles, and the lowest level of passenger revenue since 1968.

Revenue had decreased steadily from £2300-million in 1970 to £1800-million in 1982, while costs had risen from £2500-million to £2700-million. The passenger deficit was £933-million.

Meanwhile, car ownership was at an all-time high and continuing to soar year by year.

It was probably inevitable that a Conservative Government headed by Margaret Thatcher which was marked by a drive towards self sufficiently

would re-examine the rail network sooner than later.

That year, one was indeed commissioned, and produced by a committee chaired by Sir David Serpell KCB CMG OBE, a senior civil servant who had worked under none other than Dr Beeching. However, even by the standards of the junked Beeching Mark 2 report of 1965, its recommendations began at brutal and got worse from there.

BELOW Birmingham Snow Hill station saw its last trains to Wolverhampton via Smethwick withdrawn on 6 March 1972. The Great Western Hotel at the front had been demolished in 1969, and afterwards the derelict station became a car park, until most of it was knocked down in 1977

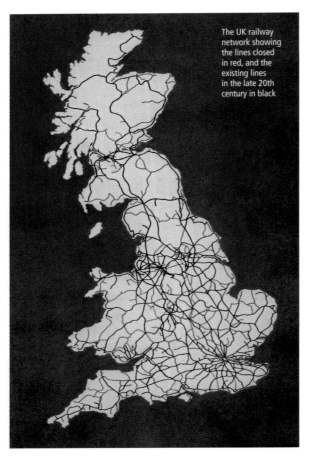

The UK railway network showing the lines closed in red, and the existing lines in the late 20th century in black

In short, the Serpell Report, correctly named Railway Finances, offered the option of reducing the 10,370 route miles of the UK network down to a skeletal network of just 1630 miles.

The bulk of the report, published in January 1983, examined in depth the state of British Rail's finances in 1982, while its second part considered a series of options and variations of them for the network as it might appear in 1992.

The first option would be to aim for a commercial network, in which the railways as a whole would make a profit. To do that, route mileage would have to be cut by a staggering 84 per cent, and annual passenger miles by 56 per cent. That would leave London-Bristol/Cardiff, London-Birmingham-Liverpool/Manchester-Glasgow/Edinburgh, and London-Leeds/Newcastle as the only main line left.

This plan would keep some of the London commuter lines in the Home Counties, but all others would close.

The lossmaking passenger sector would be subsidised by profits from the freight sector.

The second option was almost identical to the first, apart for making provision for the cost of tackling road congestion caused by rail closures. If the overall cost to the nation of closing a railway line was greater than saving it once road congestion had been considered, it would be kept. This second option would still cut route mileage by 78 per cent, and annual passenger miles by 45 per cent, keeping most of the London commuter lines.

The third option took a different tack, by offering various ways to cut the annual deficit through specific targets. One of these would have kept the existing network virtually intact, apart from the worst of the lossmaking routes and closing many smaller stations. Listed among the one per cent of the network that would close here was the Westbury-Weymouth line. Overall passenger miles would have been cut by only four per cent.

Another target suggested was to cut the annual deficit to £700 million, by closing more loss-making services such as the Tarka Line from Exeter to Barnstaple, Trowbridge-Melksham-Chippenham line, the Norwich to Cromer and Sheringham branch, the Central Wales Line and the Cambrian Coast Main Line west of Shrewsbury.

An ever harsher target would be to

THE END OF MASS CLOSURES

BELOW How Britain's railway network would have looked had the Serpell Report of 1982 been implemented

ABOVE The terminus
of the Bridport branch
in 1963, earmarked
for the Beeching Axe,
it took until 1975 for
it to close

reduce the deficit to £500 million a year. That would have seen the elimination of all lines in East Anglia apart from the line to Norwich, all routes in Wales apart from the valley lines north of Cardiff, all rural routes in Scotland, all lines in Devon and Cornwall other than the GWR main line to Exeter; the Salisbury-Exeter line, the trans-Pennine line; and most local routes east of the East Coast Main Line. This would have slashed route mileage by 39 per cent, and yearly passenger miles reduced by 15 per cent.

A fourth option would dispense with the overriding financial restraint, and keep routes serving communities with a population greater than 25,000.

The Serpell Report was immediately pounced on by rail supporters, who said that it did not consider improvements to rail services as a means of attracting passengers. It was labelled as a 'second Beeching' because of its focus on closing secondary routes.

Matters were made worse by the fact that Transport Minister David Howell, who had commissioned the report, sat on it for a month after receiving it, during which time parts were leaked to the press, generating anger and fears among commuters and the rail unions.

The government blamed British Rail for the leaks, which a grateful Labour party under Michael Foot made much of. With a general election looming, many Conservative MPs became nervous.

The popular British Rail chairman from 1976-83 Sir Peter Parker said that he found Serpell "as cosy as a razor blade". He exploited the report's suggested closures to persuade the train drivers' union ASLEF to call off a threatened strike that would have shut the rail system. Serpell, then 70, who had become permanent secretary at the Ministry of Transport in 1968, even endured personal abuse from a guard on his train home to Devon.

Largely because of the report's extremely harsh first option, it met with so much fierce resistance from many quarters that it was quickly abandoned, and there were no changes to the network made. However, it nonetheless reflected the way in which some in high places were thinking, and pre-empted the following years, in which British Rail was often accused by the unions of trying to cut costs and close lines by introducing "Serpell by stealth". The Serpell Report led to the end of Howell's ministerial career, many believed, for after the Conservatives' crushing victory in the April 1983 election, Thatcher dropped him from the cabinet.

However, passenger numbers improved through the mid and late eighties, reaching a 20-year high in 1988, and with privatisation on the horizon in 1993, the Serpell Report was consigned to history.

Serpell decided to retire for good, and moved to Dartmouth, ironically the only town in Britain with a station that famously has never had a railway running into it, for it was built on the opposite side of the river from the rail terminus at Kingswear, to which it was linked by ferry. He died on 28 July 2008 at the aged of 96.

Chapter 8

Great Beeching survivors

RIGHT The Central Wales Line is one of the greatest of all Beeching survivors. Preserved BR Standard 4MT 2-6-4T No 80079 and LMS 'Black Five' No 44767 George Stephenson are seen heading a charter into Sugar Loaf tunnel on 6 June 1993

While banner-waving protestors who gathered outside stations on the last day of services on their local line may have felt that they were wasting their breath against a Government 'one size fits all' policy, that the consultation procedures were purely academic, and that the Labour government which pledged to reverse the cuts re-engaged on that promise after it won two General Elections in 1964, several lines were reprieved sooner or later.

On 3 March 1964, nearly a year after the publication of the Beeching report, Marples announced that he had refused consent to closure in two cases – the Central Wales Line between Craven Arms, Pontardulais and Llanelli (now marketed as the Heart of Wales Line), and the Ayr-Kilmarnock line in Scotland. He did, however, agree to the closure of the southernmost branch of the Central Wales Line between Pontardulais and Swansea Victoria, from June that year.

Regarding the Central Wales Line, Marples said he had taken on board the fact that it served several towns and villages in central Wales, some of which had no other public transport and few of which had even a daily bus; it also provided a cross-country link between Swansea, west Wales and the north of England. He did accept that some stations and halts were all but unused and told the British Railways Board that he would be prepared to consider their closure.

Regarding Ayr-Kilmarnock, Marples endorsed the finding of the Scottish Transport Users Consultative Committee, but said he might reconsider in another 12 months.

Marples said that the railways' annual operating loss had been reduced by about £17-million in 1963, and that progress was being made, but un-remunerative passenger services listed by Beeching were costing the taxpayer at least £30-million in annual subsidies, a heavy burden which had to be reduced.

Marples said: "That is far from being the case. Most of my consents are not just 'yes', they are 'yes, but...'".

Some of his consents had no conditions except maintenance of existing bus services; others were consents with special requirements for extra bus services; others were consents deferred to give time for road improvements; and yet others were consents with the proviso that warning must be given if British Railways wished to take up the track.

Marples said that he was taking into account all important factors, including social considerations, the pattern of industrial development and possible effects on roads and road traffic. "They also show that in every case, I have accepted the Transport Users Consultative Committee's view on hardship almost entirely", he said. "This shows how much I rely on them. I have also nearly always accepted their proposals for extra services to relieve hardship, and sometimes I have gone further than they recommended.

"We look at everything that has a bearing on each proposal - buses, roads, traffic, regional development, commut-

ing needs, holiday travel. All the facts are brought to an official working party, on which all Government departments with relevant responsibilities are represented. They report to me, and I consider each case personally."

Marples decision on the Central Wales Line came despite observations made by the Transport Users Consultative Committee that between Llandovery and Craven Arms, only the stations at Knighton and Llandrindod Wells were taking more than £5 a day in receipts. Yet the TUCC also said that the withdrawal of services would cause considerable hardship.

Nevertheless, the line was reduced

to single track during 1964/5 as an economy measure.

A second closure threat appeared in 1967, but the line again reprieved, on social grounds.

Sceptics said that Harold Wilson saved it from closure was because it passed through six marginal constituencies.

British Rail continued to seek economies despite receiving a subsidy to operate the line, and in 1972, produced a stroke of inspiration, one which might have saved many other lines in the Beeching report. It successfully applied for a Light Railway Order under the 1896 Act for the section of the 783/4-mile section of the line between Craven Arms and Pantyffynnon, even though the line speed is 60mph and not the required 25mph. However, the order still allowed many operational procedures to be simplified and so produced economies.

The future of the line was again thrown into question in 1987 when the Glanrhyd bridge near Llandeilo collapsed after heavy flooding, and an early morning northbound diesel multiple unit plunged into the swollen River Towy, killing four people. The Carmarthen-Aberystwyth line had been closed in 1965 following serious flood damage because the cost of repairs was deemed uneconomic, but in the case of the Central Wales Line, by then there was unanimous support for the line to be saved.

Marples again saved the day

In spring 1964, Ernest Marples announced a reprieve for the heavily loss-making routes tot he north and West of Inverness, the Far North Line to Wick and Thurso and the Kyle of Lochalsh branch.

If Beeching's recommendations had been adopted, there would have been no trains north of Stirling.

ABOVE Marples refused to save the Caernarfon to Afon Wen branch. The isolated signalbox at Penygroes station is pictured after closure

However, after listening to the powerful Highland lobby, the Transport Minister agreed that that transport in the region was a special case. At the time there was no realistic prospect of alternative road transport to replace it, and the line closures could cause extreme and widespread hardship for the sake of saving £360,000 a year.

Conversely, British Railways then promised to make the services more attractive to promote greater use by both passengers and freight.

The Kyle line appeared at risk again in the seventies when the Stornaway ferry was switched to Ullapool, but tourism and again social considerations saved the day.

In September 1964, Ernest Marples sanctioned the closure of 38 passenger routes, as recommended by Beeching, but reprieved three others. These were Newcastle-Riverside-Tynemouth, the previous mentioned Middlesbrough-Whitby, and Llandudno Junction-Blaenau Ffestiniog.

He also redeemed two others, the Darlington-Bishop Auckland section of the Darlington-Crook line, along with the Bangor-Caernarfon section of the Bangor-Afon Wen route.

He stopped the closure of Newcastle-Tynemouth because it carried large numbers of workers to and from the Tyne shipyards in a badly-congested area. The Tyne & Wear Metro light rail system now links the two.

In the case of the 28-mile wonderfully-scenic Blaenau Ffestiniog line, he was swayed by both by the hardship which closure would cause to local residents, particularly in winter when the road to Blaenau over the Crimea Pass is affected by snow and ice, and also by tourism.

Nonetheless, he agreed to the closure of the stations at Glan Conwy and Dolgarrog.

From 1964, the line was used for nuclear flask traffic to Trawsfynydd power station. The GWR route from Blaenau to Bala which closed in 1961 after being flooded by Llyn Celyn reservoir was partially reopened in 1964 from Blaenau to Trawsfynydd, with a new rail connection built to link it at Blaenau to the line to Llandudno Junction. Power station traffic ceased in 1998 and that part of the line is now mothballed.

The Blaenau branch is now marketed as the Conwy Valley Line, and in 1982, opened a new interchange station with the Ffestiniog Railway in the town. Glan

Conwy and Dolgarrog have since been reopened.

Sadly, while the magnificent Conwy Valley line was reprieved, around the same time another spectacular route, the 53-mile GWR line between Ruabon and Morfa Mawddach via Bala was closed. Two sections have been reopened as heritage lines; Llangollen-Carrog (Corwen scheduled for 2012) as the standard gauge Llangollen Railway, and the length along the shores of Llyn Tegid (Lake Bala) as the 1ft 11½in gauge Bala Lake Railway.

The service between Bishop Auckland and Darlington was retained for use by large numbers of workers from Bishop Auckland travelling to work in the Darlington-Aycliffe "Growth Area". Bishop Auckland was seen as a railhead for the Crook-Tow Law region.

It not only survives today, but links to the Weardale Railway, a largely pre-Beeching passenger closure which has been revived for passenger and freight services by US operator British American Rail Services.

The Bangor-Caernarfon line was spared because Marples accepted that it provided a much better railhead than Bangor for travellers via the North Wales Coast Line to and from places farther south, including Pwllheli and the Butlin's holiday camp at Penychain.

ABOVE Preserved LMS 'Black Five' 4-6-0 No 45407 pulls into Kyle of Lochalsh station with the 'North Briton' railtour on 5 August 2006. Beeching recommended this beautiful line for closure, but today mainland ports for the Isle of Skye are served by two rail lines, the other being the West Highland extension from Fort William to Mallaig which has also warded off closure threats

GREAT BEECHING SURVIVORS

However, his successors did not share the same view.

It was closed to passenger traffic on 5 January 1970. Following the fire that severely damaged the railway bridge over the Menai Strait, the branch and Caernarfon goods yard were temporarily reopened for goods traffic from 23 May 1970 to 30 January 1972. Following closure all the track was removed and the station was completely demolished.

Caernarfon had a new station opened on 11 October 1997, but with a line running south along the trackbed of the Afon Wen route for which Marples had sanctioned closure when reprieving Bangor-Caernarfon.

It was the first part of a new Welsh Highland Railway which was being developed by the Ffestiniog Railway and which included the route of its predecessor that had closed on 5 September 1936. The completed and extended new Welsh Highland saw its first public services through to Porthmadog on 19 February 2011, and as that town has a main line station, Caernarfon can now be said to have been reconnected by rail to the national network.

The stations at Delphinine and Carr Bridge on the Perth-Inverness line were saved because they serve isolated communities largely dependent on the tourist trade, and are still open today.

Marples took the view that it would be extremely expensive to provide adequate alternative services. However, it still remains the fact that under both him and his Labour successors, far many more lines and stations to which closure objections had been raised were axed.

Settle and Carlisle

Following the closure of smaller intermediate stations in the 1960s, the Beeching report recommended the withdrawal of all passenger services from one of Britain's most scenic and best-loved routes, the Settle to Carlisle line.

The Beeching recommendations were shelved, but in May 1970 all stations apart from Settle and Appleby West were closed, and local passenger services cut to two trains a day in each direction, leaving mostly freight.

The 'Thames-Clyde Express' from London to Glasgow Central via Leicester was withdrawn in 1975, and night sleepers from London to Glasgow using the route followed the year afterwards. A residual service from Glasgow to Nottingham survived until May 1982.

It was clear that the line and its viaducts and tunnels were suffering from lack of investment, and deterioration might yet do the job of the Beeching Axe. During the 1970s, most freight traffic

BELOW Irony here as A1 Peppercorn Pacific No 60163 Tornado, a new example of the class which was rendered extinct during the scramble to dieselise in the sixties, heads through Ribblehead station, which was closed by Beeching and later reopened, the Settle & Carlisle line being reprieved in 1989

was diverted onto the electrified West Coast Main Line. As a counter measure, Dalesrail began operating services to closed stations on summer weekends in 1974, promoted by the Yorkshire Dales National Park Authority to encourage ramblers.

Yet by the early 1980s, the route handled only a handful of trains per day, and there were those who head the cogwheels turning in British Rail's mind from afar. In 1981 a protest group, the Friends of the Settle-Carlisle Line was set up to campaign against the line's closure even before it was officially announced.

Between 1983 and 1984 three closure notices were posted up by British Rail which was determined to shut the route. While the Beeching threat had been staved off, this time BR saw no

need for the line which had lost its freight, through passenger services and had a very limited local service. BR also considered Ribblehead Viaduct to be in an unsafe condition, and used it as the key reason for closure, stating that its repair or replacement could cost more than £6-million.

Freight ended in 1983, although more enthusiast steam specials were by then running over it.

As the threat of closure hung over the line, passenger use underwent a resurgence, as packed Class 47-hauled trains carried people wanting to travel the line for one last time. Annual journeys were recorded at 93,000 in 1983 when the campaign against closure began, and had shot up to 450,000 by 1989.

Plans were even drawn up in 1987

LITTLE BOOK OF **BEECHING**

to sell the line off to a private bidder. However, 22,000 signed a petition against closure, and eventually, on 11 April 1989, the recently-promoted Conservative Transport Minister

Paul Channon announced that the closure notices had been withdrawn. In 1991, work began on repairing Ribbleshead Viaduct.

The decision was the right one. While it may be easy to justify closing a line because of the current viability, how often are future traffic flows predicted, or how far can they be expected to be foreseen?

Much freight now uses the Settle and Carlisle route due to congestion on the West Coast Main Line, and includes coal from the Hunterston coal terminal in Scotland taken to power stations in Yorkshire, and gypsum from Drax Power Station carried to Kirkby Thore. Significant engineering work was needed to upgrade the line to carry such heavy freight traffic and additional investment made to reduce the length of signal sections.

The line is also used as a diversionary route from the West Coast Main Line during engineering works, while eight stations closed in 1970 were reopened.

In 2009 a bronze statue of Ruswarp, a collie dog belonging to Graham Nuttall, the first secretary of the Friends of the Settle-Carlisle Line, was unveiled on the platform of the refurbished Garsdale station. It is there to mark the saving of the line by people power, and the fact that Ruswarp is believed to be the only dog to sign a petition against a rail closure originally proposed by Beeching, or any other for that matter.

A fisherman still jolly

In October 1960, Mablethorpe & Sutton Urban District Council voiced concerns when British Railways announced its intention to close the route from Louth to Mablethorpe, the northern part of a loop serving the resort popular with East Midlands and northern families.

As most of the holiday traffic to Mablethorpe and Sutton came over the southern half of the loop via Willoughby, closure of the Louth line was seen as having little impact.

There was little opposition to the closure and the last trains ran on 3 December 1960.

Yet while the British Transport Commission said that the remaining services to Mablethorpe from the south would remain, with improved stabling facilities at the resort to facilitate an increased number of excursion trains, councillors remained fearful that within a few years that line would close too.

They were right: British Railways failed to honour pledges to develop holiday traffic to Mablethorpe and Sutton, instead reducing both services and the availability of cheap tickets. For them, it was no surprise that the Beeching report of 1963 proposed the closure of virtually the whole of the East Lincolnshire network.

Lined up for the axe was the original Great Northern railway main line from Grimsby to London via Boston and Peterborough, Lincoln–Firsby via Bardney, Willoughby-Mablethorpe and the Skegness branch.

It was the railway that had turned Skegness from a tiny village into a massive resort. The Great Northern Railway's Jolly Fisherman poster extolling the virtues of the windswept North Sea coastal town because it was so bracing became one of the most famous and successful pieces of railway advertising of all time.

Freight traffic over the Mablethorpe line was withdrawn from 30 March 1964 but opposition to the loss of the passenger services was long and bitter, with a public hearing being held in Skegness on 15/16 September 1964. By the time the hearing took place, in the case of the rundown Mablethorpe branch, British Railways was able to argue that fewer passengers were likely to suffer hardship because by then, local residents had been deterred from using the services by the reductions.

Mablethorpe and Sutton Urban District Council wanted the line to stay because it said that roads from the proposed railhead at Boston were poor or inadequate. The Minister of Transport studied the findings of the inquiry and ordered British Railways to reconsider the closure plans. It did so, and proposed the same closures, but saving the Boston to Skegness line.

A second Transport Users Consultative Committee inquiry was held at Skegness in May 1968 and this time the Transport Minister backed the requested closures. He said that while closing the Mablethorpe line would affect the summer tourist trade, as at numerous resorts elsewhere in Britain, there were not enough users of the service during the rest of the year to justify keeping the service.

The Mablethorpe line closed from 5 October 1970 and was lifted the following year.

Skegness and Boston remain linked to the national network via the route to Sleaford, Grantham and Nottingham, now rebranded and promoted as the Poacher Line. The mass influx of summer seaside specials is now consigned to history, but the Jolly Fisherman remains as the trademark of Skegness.

BELOW The famous Jolly Fisherman poster which promoted rail travel to Skegness on a branch which Beeching wanted to close

Chapter 9

Reopenings as heritage railways

Back in 1962, as we saw earlier, Dr Beeching opened a new station on the Bluebell Railway, which was the first section of the British Railways main line network to be closed and then reopened as a private venture by volunteers and enthusiasts. Today, such heritage railways account for a major slice of Britain's tourist industry.

From such small beginnings, there are 108 operating railways and 60 more steam centres in the British Isles. Laid end to end, they would total 510 miles with 399 stations, a greater route mileage than that of the London Underground system and longer than the distance between London and Glasgow. More heritage railways are being planned.

In 2009, heritage railways and muse-ums carried 6.7-million passengers and earned around £81-million. They directly employ around 2000 people and are backed up by an army of nearly 18,000 volunteers and many, many more armchair supporters.

Many of them run over routes that Beeching closed, and yet are showing an operating profit, which his almost always ploughed back into infrastructure, or breaking even.

Therefore, does this not show that Beeching got his sums wrong?

By no means – in fact, quite the opposite.

When many branch lines were axed in the early sixties, often communities which had rallied round in vain to try to save them subsequently looked at taking them over by themselves. A classic

example is the Keighley & Worth Valley Railway, where the entire five-mile branch from Keighley to Oxenhope was saved by the local community and after reopening in 1968, went on to worldwide fame as the setting for the EMI film of Edith A Nesbit's children's classic The Railway Children.

Yet how many of them ever managed to run conventional daily public services round the year, as opposed to seasonal tourist lines showcasing restored heritage steam and diesel locomotives and rolling stock?

The answer is not many. Not even a handful.

On 5 April 1969, after the Dart Valley Railway bought the line from British Rail, the first preservation era trains ran over the Ashburton branch in Devon from Buckfastleigh to a point near the main line junction north of Totnes, under the new operator's Light Railway Order, with GWR pannier tank No 6412.

This heritage line was officially opened by none other than axeman Dr Richard Beeching himself – even though it was not one of the many branches that he had infamously closed.

However, in another twist to the battle between road and rail, the revivalists failed to persuade the Ministry of Transport not to take the top portion of the route, the two-mile stretch from Buckfastleigh to Ashburton, for use as part of the new A38 dual carriageway trunk road from Exeter to Plymouth, and therefore the entire branch was not saved, as had been the case with the KWVR.

The year before, British Rail had announced its intention to close the seven-mile Paignton to Kingswear section of the branch from Newton Abbot, in many ways a main line in all but name.

Many eyebrows were raised when the Dart Valley Railway successfully bidded to buy it, taking it over from British Rail in service, without any 'last day' trains and the like associated with the Beeching closures.

The line was bought as a going concern on 30 January 1972, the purchase price being £250,000 with a further £25,000 paid for signalling alterations at Paignton. Most of this was recouped from the sale of the Royal Dart Hotel at Kingswear and other surplus land.

A new independent station was built at Paignton Queen's Park alongside the British Rail station to serve the Kingswear trains and a winter service was run from 1 January 1973.

However, the operating figures did not stack up for either British Rail or the new owners. It quickly became clear that the Dart Valley Railway could not afford to run a daily service round the year, and so from the end of summer 1973 it became a purely seasonal operation.

Dart Valley Railway plc found that the glorious coastal scenery reaped big dividends, while as the years wore on, the original Buckfastleigh line incurred losses. To cut a very long story short, the Buckfastleigh line was eventually sold to the line's volunteer supporters association, which had rebranded

it as the South Devon Railway, and thanks to freely-given labour, very much flourishes today. Meanwhile, the Paignton-Kingswear line, now branded the Dartmouth Steam railway and River Boat Company, is the only heritage line in Britain to pay annual dividends to its shareholders, relying on paid staff and having built up a transport empire including a boat fleet.

ABOVE GWR 2-8-0 No 3803, on loan from the South Devon Railway, departs from Toddington on the Gloucestershire Warwickshire Railway. Father's Day June 2010

ABOVE Several lines closed by Dr Beeching have been revived as narrow gauge tourist railways. Who would have guessed from this 2008 view of Quarry Hunslet 0-4-0 saddle tank Lilian that the Launceston Steam railway lies on the route of the fabled 'Atlantic Coast Express' which ran from Waterloo to Padstow until the sixties

A revived line earmarked for closure for Beeching was the Minehead branch, known today as the West Somerset Railway, reopened in stages between Minehead and the first original station on the branch proper, Bishops Lydeard, between 1976-79, it tried to run regular services for local people, using classic diesel multiple units painted in 1950s carmine and cream livery. The figures also did not stack up here, and the line was hampered by not being allowed to run over the main line into Taunton,

as did the branch trains under the GWR and British Railways.

Although the main line connection at Norton Fitzwarren still existed, one reason given in the early eighties was that it would make a connecting bus service between Taunton and Bishops Lydeard obsolete, and unions would object to its driver being made redundant.

Other heritage lines will argue that they have provided 'real' public transport as opposed to tourist or heritage trains. The 15in gauge Romney Hythe & Dymchurch Railway, long billed as a main line in miniature, has run regular school trains for local youngsters. The Swanage Railway, which managed to rebuild half the London & South Western Railway branch line from the resort westwards, was hailed as a huge success because of the park-and-ride facility at its eastern terminus of Norden was credited with easing summer congestion on the A351, the spine road of the Isle of Purbeck.

Yet the reality is that none of them have replicated the services that ended under Beeching and British Railways, despite the provision of volunteer labour to maintain both rolling stock and infrastructure. What has been produced by preservationists is magnificent beyond belief, giving new generations an insight into the glory days of Britain's railway past and the chance to ride behind steam engines once again polished to perfection, but each of them is a very different animal to the running of a regular public timetable service 362 days a year.

If, of course, a local authority was to step in and subsidise running commuter or shopper services on these lines, it would be a different matter indeed. With fears of a global fuel crisis in 2011 and a growing desire to conserve the environment and avoid traffic congestion, fresh new opportunities may well arise here.

Yet how far has any heritage railway revival scheme proved Beeching wrong?

Yet, if it were possible to run seaside branch lines only during the summer season, many more could have been saved, but Beeching would be quick to point out the enormous cost of storing and maintaining the rolling stock for the rest of the time when it would not be used, as well as that of maintaining the route infrastructure throughout the year. In any age where the car is king, such figures would never stack up.

A moonlight flit to France

And what of Ernest Marples, the Transport Minister who, not Beeching, made the ultimate decision to close a third of Britain's railways?

Road builder Marples, who had spent his younger days working as a miner, a postman, a chef and an accountant, becoming an army captain during World War Two, elected to Parliament as conservative MP for Wallasey in 1945, and Postmaster General in 1957, retired from the House of Commons at the February 1974 general election. Three months later, his public service was rewarded when he was made a life peer as Baron Marples of Wallasey.

In early 1975, before the end of the tax year, Marples fled without warning to the tax haven of Monaco, by the night ferry with his belongings packed into tea chests, after fighting off a reassessment of his financial assets.

ABOVE GWR 0-6-0 pannier tank No 6412 heads out of Wansford across the River Nene towards Peterborough during a loan visit to the Nene Valley Railway

It was said that he had formulated a plot to remove £2-million from Britain through his Liechtenstein company. He claimed he had been asked to pay unpaid tax dating back three decades.

After he had gone, discarded clothes and possessions were found scattered over the floors of his Belgravia home.

The late Fleet Street editor Richard Stott, when investigating Marples' flight to France, was told by him: "You are the worst journalist I have ever met. The most aggressive man I have ever met in my life."

The comment, of which Stott was immensely proud, was highlighted in the programme for the journalist's memorial service at St Clement Danes in the Strand on 30 July 2007 after he died at the age of 63.

The Government froze Marples' remaining assets in Britain for the next 10 years, but most of his fortune had by then been squirreled away to Monaco and Lichtenstein. He never returned to Britain, and spent the rest of his life in his French chateau at Fleurie, where he owned a vineyard, dying on 6 July 1978 in the Princess Grace Hospital Centre in Monaco.

It has since been claimed that when the late Lord Denning investigated the security aspects of the Profumo Affair in 1963, he told Prime Minister Harold Macmillan that a similar contemporary rumour, one concerning Marples, appeared to be true. Journalists claimed that the story was suppressed and was omitted from Denning's final report, but we will probably never know whether there is any truth in such claims.

LEFT LMS 'Jinty' 3F 0-6-0T No 47279 departs from Stoneacre loop with a train from Bolton Abbey on the Embsay & Bolton Abbey Steam Railway

BOTTOM LEFT Cadeleigh station on the Exe Valley line which was closed on 7 October 1963 is now the Devon Railway Centre, where a 2ft gauge line has been laid on part of the trackbed as a tourist attraction. In August 2010, three Kerr Stuart Wren class 0-4-0STs were seen in operation

Chapter 10

The final verdict

RIGHT Preserved
B1 4-6-0 No 61264
calls at Stamford
in August 2006.
Beeching's 1963
report recommended
the closure of local
stopping services
on the Leicester to
Peterborough line,
and accordingly, in
1966 intermediate
village stations
such as Ketton &
Collyweston and
Helpston closed

So what should we really make of Dr Beeching today, 50 years after he became British Railways chairman and "the most hated civil servant in Britain".

Was he a bogeyman – or a benefactor? If we long for the steam era through rose-tinted spectacles, and long for the days when country towns and villages were served by a dense network of cross-country routes and branch lines, which meant that you could travel almost anywhere by train, then he will be damned without redemption by our sentimentality, and we should read no further.

Likewise, if we view the relationship between Transport Minister Ernest Marples, who had vested interests in road building and ended up fleeing Britain with vast unpaid tax bills, and the man he chose to pay a near-popstar salary bring hard-hitting business principles to British Railways at a time when it was plunging ever deeper into a mire of unprecedented debt, we might be forgiven for thinking that dark forces of self interest conspired to bring about the demise of the national network that was, in favour of alternative transport.

Understandably, there was no love lost between Beeching and the tens of thousands of lowly-paid rail workers who were left on the scrap heap with meagre pensions by the cutbacks which they considered to be vindictive and impersonal to their dying day, accusing him of mercilessly wielding his axe with vitriol, glee and even spite.

In 1962, there were 474,536 people employed by British Railways – the figure fell to around 307,000 by 1968.

Yet Beeching could not be blamed for their historic low wages and the inherited hopeless level of overstaffing on lines for which public demand was disappearing fast – and maybe their venom might instead have been better directed at former rail passengers who had bought a car.

However, if we place everything in its true context, we must look outside the bubble that is Britain.

The hard fact is that countries throughout the western hemisphere had been closing unremunerative lines since the 1930s. What was happening in Britain in the fifties and sixties was also taking place in North America, the continent, where swathes of rural metre gauge lines were being closed, and closer to home, Ireland. Countries like the USA were years ahead of Britain in terms of dieselisation, electrification and route rationalisation.

Everywhere, those in power were also having to come to grips with the unparalled phenomenon of the soaring levels of private motor transport, from motorbikes to luxury cars. It was certainly not a problem limited to Britain, and likewise Beeching and Marples cannot be blamed for the closure trends in other countries. Indeed, global evidence indicates that closures at this time were unavoidable.

Dr Richard Beeching was awarded a controversial salary typical of the higher-paid private sector than a civil servant. He was also given a remit, which broadly said that the deficit must be cut at all costs, and he was given scant leeway to recommend that loss-making lines should be retained on social grounds. Such judgement was ultimately left to Marples, who did redeem some routes recommended for the axe by Beeching, and who has also been accused of delaying other closures as the 1964 General Election loomed.

The hard fact is that some railway lines running in the fifties and sixties should never have been built at all, because they had been designed and built more than a century ago in starkly different socio-economic conditions, with hope of riches that never materialised.

Other lines had become so poorly patronised that it would have been cheaper to pay for the daily users to share a taxi.

Take the GWR's Cheltenham to Kingham and Banbury route, for instance. How many people would travel daily to Cheltenham or Banbury from, say, Bourton-on-the Water or Chipping Norton? Take away the line's coal and agricultural traffic, and what business case do you have left?

One often-expounded argument against Beeching was the failure to recognise the full importance loss leaders. Closing any branch line eradicated its traffic contribution to the main line. In fact, this aspect was addressed in The Reshaping of British Railways, although his response was not as flexible as it might have been.

Beeching and others assumed that disenfranchised villagers would merely use motor transport to reach the nearest main line station, and so often they were proved wrong.

On the other hand, by the early sixties many remote branch lines had so few regular passengers that their revenue contribution to the main line was negligible, and in these cases, it is difficult to argue with Beeching.

The savings that Beeching promised to make never materialised. By closing almost a third of the network, he managed to achieve a saving of just £30-million, while overall losses were still above £100-million.

His 'Mark 2' report in 1965 which caused for even more drastic closures, disenfranchising large regions as well as towns and village from the network, was such an embarrassment that he parted company with British Railways soon after, ahead of schedule.

Yet if the rationale behind the 1963 report was so wrong, why did Harold Wilson's Labour Government which had publicly pledged to stop the Beeching cuts before winning the General Election in 1964 not only immediately renege on its promises, but in some cases speeded up the closures.

Labour Transport Minister Barbara Castle introduced a key social element which led to the potential retention of unviable lines, and set in place the Passenger Transport Executive model by which integrated urban transport could be – as happened successfully – developed, but let us not forget she still closed thousands of miles of routes as recommended by Beeching

LEFT A typical but rarely-photographed post-Beeching scene: the goods yard at Alston being demolished after the withdrawal of goods services in September 1966. The passenger platform is still intact beyond the Drott bulldozer working in the ruins of the goods shed. The Alston-Haltwhistle passenger service escaped the immediate axe and lasted until May 3 1976 due to poor road connections in the area. Alston is now the terminus of the 2ft gauge South Tynedale Railway

and then added several more routes into the bargain. A strong element of the recognition of the fact that widespread closures in a car-dominated country inevitable appears here.

In a great decade of change, when the steam era that had served the country so well during two world wars was visibly disappearing, with new futuristic forms of transport jumping off the drawing board, and where the car provided a liberating force to even modest income families, there were those who believed that modernised or not, the days of the railways were numbered.

John Sergeant's view of Beeching

In spring 2011, veteran television reporter John Sergeant used Scotland's Bo'ness & Kinneil Railway as a backdrop to an item on the Beeching Cuts he recorded for BBC's The One Show.

A special train hauled by Class 26 diesel No 26024 did two trips from Bo'ness to Birkhill to allow the film crew to get "the train in motion effect" while John did an interview.

Travelling with John was rail expert David Spaven who provided detailed examples of how the cuts savaged the UK network by about a third.

John said: "We think of Beeching as being a bad guy. We think, looking back, if we hadn't had this guy, lots of lovely railways could have been preserved.

"But it was very much a problem of the time and people thought that railways then were old fashioned and they were uneconomic. So something had to be done – and that was a savage reappraisal of the entire railway network.

"My conclusion is that Beeching is neither a hero nor a villain but very much a man of his time."

The biggest failing of all

For me, the biggest mistake of the Beeching era and the years that followed was the speed and ruthlessness by which closures were implemented, leaving little possibility of going back should circumstances change – as they have done.

New towns were appearing on the landscape, and with inner-city redevelopment, sizeable communities were springing up on the outskirts of cities. Meanwhile, country towns and villages that previously could not support their local branch line would eventually add housing estates and become much-sought-after commuter belt settlements.

With soaring levels of car ownership, surely it was obvious that rush-hour gridlock in cities would occur within the foreseeable future, and buses without dedicated lanes would fare no better than cars in jams. Where there are bus lanes, they so often serve the purpose of slowing cars to snail's pace in the remaining lane – often people need their car for their job, and using public transport is not an option.

Countries like France got it right. Yes, withdraw the worst lossmaking services, but keep the trackbed, if not the track itself, intact for potential future use should circumstances change.

In Britain, such options were discarded too quickly or never even considered, tracks being lifted sometimes within days of closure leaving no going back, and the land sold off.

The problem is that any land that is sold off in urban areas will be sooner rather than later redeveloped. The cost of repurchasing former railway land in cities and demolishing buildings in the way of any reinstatement schemes immediately makes most of them non-viable. Building new termini on the edges of urban areas rather than in their centres defeats the object.

What had long rankled with me is the case of the closure of the GWR Stratford-upon-Avon to Cheltenham line, which in post-Beeching years had been retained for freight. In 1976, more than a decade after Beeching, a derailment at Chicken Curve near Winchcombe damaged the track and led to a British Rail decision not to bother repairing the line. Most of the 28-mile route was lifted three years later, and the trackbed through Stratford used for a town bypass, although a grass strip capable of accommodating a single track was left.

Fast forward a third of a century, and the houses now built around the site in Stratford have changed hands many times. While in the late nineties, Network Rail's predecessor Railtrack was seriously looking at reopening the route for freight as a bypass for the Lickey Incline, I have no doubt that there would now be an overwhelming 'not in my back yard' protest, as well as problems with crossing the new roadway on the level.

Had the trackbed been preserved intact, while letting everyone know that the railway might come back one day, this situation and many others like it would be avoided.

I once looked at badly-gridlocked Bath, and attempts being made to regenerate the former coalmining towns of Radstock and Midsomer Norton. Why not, I wondered, reinstate the Somerset & Dorset main line linking all three, as a commuter route, so people could buy cheap housing and commute to Bath and Bristol? I was informed as a rough estimate that it would cost at least as much in actual pounds (forgetting inflation) to rebuild that section of line as Beeching managed to save by closing an entire third of Britain's rail network.

What if?

What if Dr Richard Beeching had never been appointed in 1961?

The regions of British Railways would certainly have closed more and more branch lines as they had been doing for several years, probably without any reference to a central guiding criteria.

Allowing them to carry on doing

LEFT GWR prairie tank No 5541 heads a train at Tavistock South on 16 June 1962. The last passenger trains from Launceston to Plymouth via Tavistock were scheduled to run on 29 December 1962, the closure to passengers taking effect from the following Monday, 31 December. However, heavy snowfalls quashed any bid to commemorate the end of the GWR branch. The 6.20am Plymouth terminated at Tavistock at 12.20am the following day, while the 7.10am Tavistock to Plymouth was stranded at Bickleigh overnight, nature holding off the end for another day. Beeching had a point here, because this route largely mirrored the Southern Railway main line from Plymouth to Exeter, but that also closed, in 1968. In 2011, talks were underway about rebuilding the latter route south to Bere Alston, re-enfranchising a town with more than 11,000 inhabitants

their own thing may have ended up with the network's finances in an even greater mess, and maybe lead to more closures than were recommended by the Beeching report.

It is worth pausing for a minute, looking back on the maps in this volume, and then seriously asking – how many of the Beeching closures would have happened in the sixties anyway, with or without him?

Similarly, another person in Beeching's place might well have closed more lines sooner, before the subsequent and enlightened social need policies of later years could save them.

Furthermore, if the recommended cutbacks had not been made at the time, and the British Railways deficit left to spiral further out of control, with only vain hopes being thrown at it, would the delay have ultimately led to far more drastic rationalisation being imposed, such as that outlined in the horror story that was the Serpell report in 1982, and with the full blessing of the over-burdened taxpayer? We will never know.

Nothing anyone could have done would have prevented the rise of the car and the mass exodus of passengers from rail to road, which offers greater personal flexibility. It was a global phenomenon, not unique to Britain.

What was being attempted by Beeching, however, was the identification of instances where passengers would still prefer to travel by train, as well as cases where the carriage of freight by rail offered clear advantages over road haulage. While there may have been elements of tunnel vision in both the remit he was given by Ernest Marples and his approach, he made an honest attempt to achieve these goals and thereby save the railway network from a far dire predicament.

He applied a simple business principle. A factory employs 20 men on the production line. Suddenly someone invents machinery that can do the job of 19 of them, leaving just one to oversee it. That one position is what may then be termed a 'real' job – it is essential for production to be maintained and cannot be replaced by technology, and the other 19 should therefore be made redundant, according to the accountant's recommendation.

The accountant's remit by nature is ruthless and cannot involve consideration as to whether sacking the 19 would cause hardship, or the loss of their incomes would have a negative effect on the local economy outside and so on. That final decision is up to the factory owners.

In the case of British Railways, Beeching was the accountant, and the owners were the Conservative and Labour Governments. The buck stopped with them.

However, if the powers that be outside the firm look at the redundancies in a wider context, such as the cost of unemployment benefit, retraining, supporting local business deprived of income from the workers who have lost their wage, and so on, they might well decide that a subsidy to the factory to retain some of the jobs, maybe in the event of increased production at a later date, would serve the local economy well.

No country has been able to support a large railway network of its original size and a modern road network side by side.

Economies were inevitable, but who knows what lines might have been saved if the social aspect of closures had been more fully addressed by transport ministers some years before Barbara Castle's 1968 Act, maybe even as soon as the pledge-breaking Harold Wilson came to power in 1964?

For a man accused of trying to destroy Britain's railways, Beeching's innovations regarding bulk freight such as the Merry-Go-Round coal hoppers and the Freightliner container system proved highly successful and are still in

use nearly half a century on.

So much changed in the sixties, including the nationalised railway network, which emerged from the decade streamlined and slimmed down, even if it was never as sleek and shiny as those who told us that the seventies were 'The Age of the Train' in TV advertising would have had us believe.

Yes, rationalisation could and almost certainly should have been done better, and while the sixties promised so much hope and optimism, the decade came packaged with liberal lashings of naiveté and lack of real foresight in so many cases.

Nonetheless, the reduced railway network has managed to ride the storm of threats to its existence like the Serpell report, and with the opening of the High Speed 1 Channel Tunnel rail link to the award-winning St Pancras International station, and the promise of a new high-speed rail link from London to Birmingham, Manchester and the north, and an east-to-west cross-link line beneath London, and passenger figures at their highest in many decades, the future for rail is now looking more promising than at any time since the 1955 Modernisation Plan.

We all miss the rural branch lines, look at them wistfully in magazines like Heritage Railway and on archive cine footage, and we know that the closure of trunk routes like the Great Central was short sighted. Too many large towns became cut off from the network, and not enough emphasis was placed on the fear that motor transport would at the rate of expansion bring cities to gridlock sooner than later.

Yet evidence, backed by a mountain

ABOVE Closures of loss-making line were going full steam ahead on throughout the UK in the fifties and sixties – and Dr Beeching had no control over any of them. Waiting to leave the terminus of the doomed Warrenpoint branch in Ulster with a return Sunday outing to Belfast on 30 August 1964 was Class S 4-4-0 No 48

RIGHT GWR 4-6-0
No 6003 King
George IV stands at
Wolverhampton Low
Level, which closed
to through trains in
1967 and completely
in 1972

of hindsight, shows that while Beeching made mistakes, he appeared to honestly and efficiently follow a given remit, albeit one that was too brutal in parts.

The cutbacks, while largely inevitable, may also be viewed as having reshaped Britain's railways into a slimmer, fitter beast that at last, after disappointing decades in the doldrums, is now gearing up to the fresh challenges of the 21st century, able to hold its head high in an age where the car will forever remain king.

Yes, it is so easy to make Dr Beeching a scapegoat, especially when you take into account the speed and clinical efficiency in which he went about his deficit-cutting task. He merely took the queen's shilling and carried out the duties he was given by not one but two democratically-elected Governments, on both sides of the political fence.

In trying to make sense of global transport trends at the beginning of the greatest decade of change, the like of which had never been seen before, he steadfastly and determinedly tackled a job which under no circumstances was ever likely to bring him universal popularity, and led to him taking the public rap for the final decisions of those in higher authority on both sides of the political fence, both during and after his term in office.

Maybe this particular hatchet man erred more of the side of the heroic than any of us want to believe.

Baron Beeching lived in Lewes Road, East Grinstead, from the 1960s until he died at Queen Victoria Hospital in 1985.

Beeching Way in East Grinstead was named after him as it lies on the route of one of the lines made obsolete by his report.

He first developed signs of heart trouble in 1969. The following year, he became chairman of building materials group Redland plc, and later became chairman of ship owners Furness Withy.

When once asked about his career with the railways, and if he regretted his cuts, he famously and somewhat pompously said that he regretted not having closed more lines. He maintained this stance to the end.

The Bluebell Railway, where as we saw in Chapter 3, he opened a new halt in 1962, months before the publication of The Reshaping of British Railways, was in 2011 steaming ahead with plans to complete its northern extension to rejoin the main line at East Grinstead, where a new station is being developed. Irony abounds from many angles.

The pictures in this book were provided courtesy of the following:

COLOUR-RAIL.COM, REDLAND PLC/COURTESY, NRM PICTORIAL COLLECTION, IAN ALLAN, ROBIN JONES, K FAIREY, ALAN EARNSHAW COLLECTION, DEREK CROSS/RM, ANDREW MUCKLEY/RM, HUGH BALLANTYNE, HARRY SHIPLER, BRIAN SHARPE, CREATIVE COMMONS, RL KNIGHT, BEAMISH MUSEUM, T E WILLIAMS/NRM, PRESS ASSOCIATION, DEREK CROSS/RM, LONDON TRANSPORT MUSEUM/TRANSPORT FOR LONDON, MIDLAND RAILWAY TRUST, BLUEBELL ARCHIVES, BRIAN MORRISON, THE MAIDSTONIAN, D LOVELOCK/RM, WA CAMWELL/RM, PB TAYLOR/RM, GREAT WESTERN TRUST, SOUTH WEST TRAINS, MIKE ESAU, DAVID BURROWS, P PAULTER/RM, PASSENGER TRANSPORT EXECUTIVE GROUP, JOHN CLARKE/RM, PHIL BARNES, ROGER DIMMICK/FR, FRIENDS OF THE SETTLE-CARLISLE LINE, CHRIS DIXON, JOHN BRODRIBB, JONATHAN MANN/LSR, HENDY POLLOCK/STRATHSPEY RAILWAY, SEATON TRAMWAY, RW COLE/RM, AA

*Note: Pictures Credited RM are reproduced courtesy of The Railway Magazine Archives

Design & Artwork: ALEX YOUNG

Published by: DEMAND MEDIA LIMITED

Publisher: JASON FENWICK

Written by: ROBIN JONES